DAUGHTERS OF THE EARTH

DAUGHTERS OF THE EARTH

Women and Land in Uttar Pradesh

SMITA TEWARI JASSAL

MANOHAR
2001

First published 2001

ISBN 81-7304-375-2

Published by
Ajay Kumar Jain for
Manohar Publishers & Distributors
4753/23 Ansari Road, Daryaganj
New Delhi 110002

Printed at
Rajkamal Electric Press
B 35/9 GT Karnal Road Indl Area
Delhi 110033

For my sons

Aftab and Nirvikar

Je kuchh arajihe e Baba, adhiya hamar
Adhiya adhiya jani kara Beti
Sabhe dhan tohar.
Chutki bhar sindurwa e Beti
Tu ta jayebu kauna paar.

In all you earn father, I stake a claim for half
Insist not on half your share daughter
This entire wealth to you belongs.
Just a pinch of vermilion daughter
And before long, far and away you'll be gone.

—Bhojpuri marriage song

Contents

	Acknowledgements	9
	Introduction	11
1.	Land, Caste and Gender: Some Hypotheses	33
2.	Peasant Differentiation in Awadh: Making Women Visible	65
3.	Custom, Legislation and Landownership: Where are the Women?	87
4.	Saga of the State, a Village and Landless Women	112
5.	Women's Marginalization: Tales from Bundelkhand	144
6.	Summing Up	167
	Appendices	173
	Glossary	177
	Bibliography	181
	Index	191

Acknowledgements

I would like to record a debt of gratitude to Vina Mazumdar who first encouraged me to work on this problematic way back in 1985. In many ways the foundation of the present enquiry was laid between 1985 and 1987, when I worked as Coordinator for a project on Women's Land Rights at the Centre for Women's Development Studies (CWDS). For the wonderful work atmosphere provided by Vinadi and Lotika Sarkar and for the thought-provoking and stimulating discussions at the Centre which shaped my thinking, I am most grateful. It has been a privilege to share in the vision of these two extraordinary women. Sections of this book draw upon my unpublished doctoral thesis for which, my PhD. supervisor at the Department of Sociology, Delhi School of Economics, S.D. Badgaiyan, deserves heartfelt thanks. I am grateful to him, Andre Beteille, and Harold Gould for discussions which helped to understand socio-historical processes in Awadh and Faizabad—it was inspiring and stimulating to share my discoveries with them!

Many individuals have read and commented on various drafts, sections and chapters of the manuscript. I particularly wish to thank Neeladri Bhattacharya for his insightful comments. Patricia Oberoi and my colleagues, Vasanthi Raman, Indu Agnihotri, Leela Kasturi and Malavika Karlekar offered detailed comments, providing feedback and support as the book progressed. I thank them all. For his suggestions on later drafts which sharpened the book's focus, I warmly thank Arun Kumar.

The book has benefited greatly from my association with the Abhiyan Samiti for Land Reforms and Labour Rights in UP. Through this network many individuals enriched my understanding of contemporary land relations there. While it is not possible to thank all of them, I wish to record my appreciation of Hazari Singh Pankaj for his depth of information and insights on rural Banda. I thank Mahanth Maurya and Kailash Nathji for introducing me to

Sarai Mohana, and extend my warmest thanks to all the village informants who made my field visits so richly rewarding.

Rinju Rasailly provided cheerful and meticulous assistance during part of the research. Nandan, Neeru and Sapna were always helpful with secretarial assistance. For their cooperation, I thank the staff of the libraries at the Centre for Women's Development Studies, the Nehru Memorial Museum, Ratan Tata Library, the National Archives of India, the UP State Archives and the Office of the Board of Revenue, Lucknow, the Faizabad Collectorate, and the India Office Library, London. In their own unique ways Carla Borden, Smita Purushottam, Ritu and Raj Kumar Singh, Mani Singh Mamik, Amita, Prabhat Shukla and Jatin Das have enriched this work.

The support provided in countless ways by my late father, J.N. Tewari, and my mother Kiran has been invaluable in my academic career. This book however, would not have been completed but for the generosity, interest and infectious enthusiasm of Raminder, my husband. It is to him and to my two sons, Aftab and Nirvikar that it rightfully belongs. They have all shared these ideas, grown with them and patiently waited for the book's completion so I could join them!

SMITA TEWARI JASSAL

INTRODUCTION

Women' Rights to Land: Socio-Historical Probings

Things we despise

Slaving for others (*ghulami*)
Erratic conditions of waged work
Landlessness
Violence within and outside the home

Changes we seek

Dignity (*izzat*)
Liberty to sell what we produce
Control over our earnings
Freedom to act without the permission of husbands

Scheduled caste and landless women
of Naugaṛh, Varanasi (13 October 1999)

In Naugarh, a remote forest region of Chandauli district near Varanasi, a group of thirty Chamar, Musahar and Kol tribe women voice their understanding of the connection between insecurity, impoverishment, dependence and oppression at the hands of government functionaries (particularly forest officials) and their landless, assetless status on the lowest rungs of the agrarian class and caste hierarchies. A few *bighas* of arable land in their own names, they unanimously conclude, will bring about the much desired liberating change from dependence on males within households as well as chronic economic and social insecurity. Women's perceptions are changing with heightened restrictions placed by the forest department on access to and mobility within the forest, which had hitherto provided survival in the face of shrinking resources and work opportunities. In several pockets throughout

UP where conditions are exploitative, or where peoples' struggles for land, resources and secure tenancies are under way, women are raising significant questions about entitlement and access to a range of resources, including land. Such questions are a first step towards challenging a social order that has systematically excluded women from ownership and control over land and productive resources, and the resultant gendered nature of the distribution of power.

Here the struggle for land has acquired greater momentum as women are beginning to see their stakes in the struggle. Landlessness is acute in the region, with miniscule holdings of 10 *biswas* which, being inadequate for family subsistence, require that both men and women of the household seek wage labour. Opportunities for the latter are few and confined to not more than two months a year in the harvest season. As migrant labour from Palamu, Bihar, is cheaper, local agricultural labourers find themselves in competition for scarce jobs and at daily wages many notches below the minimum daily wage, women receiving a wage about 20 per cent below that of males for the same work. For the major part of the year, the landless subsist on the collection and sale of firewood, a survival option that is now being closed by the forest department. For those whose ancestral lands or homes fall within the boundary of the forest, and indeed close to 90 villages are thus located, insecurity has multiplied, as villagers face eviction and coercion in the form of uprooting or harvesting of standing crops by forest officials. The systematic closure of survival options has escalated the struggle for land.

In addition to the oppression meted out by the forest department, women, particularly widows, are witness to the exploitative face of the state in the implementation of the government pensions and poverty alleviation schemes wherein a range of functionaries from the BDO to the tehsil office take substantial monetary cuts, with the result that only a small percentage of the sum in question actually reaches the allottee. For women, lack of power in the public domain is compounded in the private sphere as they experience powerlessness within house-holds, exercising little control over their own earnings or autonomy in decisions relating to household expenditure or the sale of agricultural produce.

More than thirty women from a cluster of neighbouring villages participated in a workshop held in Naugarh to discuss these issues. In articulating the necessity for rights in land, the women argued that instead of the traditional patrilineal form of inheritance, a really beneficial arrangement from their point of view would be to have title over at least some land which could then be passed on to either the son or daughter, whoever administered to their needs in old age. As things stand, some women pointed out, sons inherit the land but often ill-treat or drive out old and widowed mothers. Other women were convinced that when *pattas* are distributed to the landless, for homesteads or agricultural plots, the names of wives should be included in the title deeds along with those of husbands.

During discussions, women broke up into groups to confer with each other and came up with the suggestion that to feed a family of five for a year without undertaking any other wage work, 5 *bighas* of double-cropped arable land would be required. The women grappled with the issues of understanding and explaining the historicity of land tenure in the region, the persistence of feudal and caste oppression, and the need to challenge the structures of male privilege by demanding a share in property. And finally at the end of the two-day session, women were convinced of the need to act collectively, form *sangathans*, and if need be, march to Delhi to press their demands for land.

In the 1990s along with the negative impact of processes escalated by the New Economic Policy, there is also a distinct articulation of peasant women's voices throughout the country, through grass-roots women's organizations. It is against this backdrop that the relevance and scope of the issue of rights to land for women has to be assessed (Mazumdar 1997: 375-88).

The concerns the Naugarh women expressed during the discussions, are the themes of this book. Today, more than 85 per cent of UP's rural population is engaged in agriculture, and of the total number of agicultural labourers, more than half are women. In most areas, women receive a lower wage than men, despite the fact that apart from ploughing, they carry out a whole range of agricultural activities: sowing, reaping, weeding, threshing and processing, in addition to household duties. Yet women having title to land either as owners or tenants are few unless they are widows or single women. The understanding that women are part of the household and therefore have no right to separate entitlement, still conditions official discourse. How this bias has worked to the detriment of women's status has formed the subject of several studies.

THE PROBLEMATIC

Har hoi goyende khet hoi chas
Nari hoi gihithini bhains sanhar
Rahari ke daal jadahan ke bhat
Gaaral nebua au ghiva tat.
Saras anda dahi jab hoye
Banke nayan parosay joye
Kahe Ghagh ee saanch na jhoonth
Uhan chhadi ehawen Baikunth.

Ploughing taking place close to the village,
Fields ready for ploughing
The woman, a competent housekeeper
Lactacting buffalo
Arahar daal
Boiled new rice, a squeeze of lemon on it
And hot ghee
Curds the colour of crane's eggs
Coquettish glances from the woman who serves,
Ghagh says, this is the truth
Forget about the other one, this is real paradise!

D. Singh, 1958, *Bhojpuri ke Kavi aur Kavya*,
Patna: Bihar Rashtrabhasha Parishad (74)

Naskat panahi, batkat joye
Jo pahilaunthi bitiya hoye
Patar khet, bauraha bhaiy
Ghagh kahen dukha kahan samaye.

Shoes that pinch, woman who interrupts conversation (i.e. one with her own views)
The first born, a daughter
Low quality land
Deranged brother
If all these are present, pain knows no bounds.

D. Singh, 1958, *Bhojpuri ke Kavi aur Kavya*,
Patna: Bihar Rashtrabhasha Parishad (76)

My concern in this book is to examine women's relationship to land from the historical, anthropological and socio-legal perspectives.

The central question governing the enquiry is: how did it come about that peasant women who are known to have initiated agriculture, and continue to be actively involved in agricultural production, remain so marginalized in the ownership and control of land? In this sense do all women constitute a class vis-à-vis men or should women be seen as an integral and constituent element of castes and classes and thus differentially placed with regard to access to land? The place of women within the structures of caste and class largely determines the extent and nature of their access to land as a productive resource. The question of their rights to land therefore needs to be contextualized within familial, caste, class and power structures within the distinct social formations being considered.

This study adopts a two-pronged approach using historical and participatory methods to analyse the processes by which women have been denied land. It has been long recognized that women were the initiators of the first agricultural revolution and that they initiated rice production (Swaminathan 1985). The present enquiry is prompted by the need to address questions relating to the marginalization of women within the power and resource systems that govern agriculture, forestry and the allied sectors, and the technologies and sciences associated with the development of these as well as the social perceptions that have obscured the linkage between peasant women, natural resource management and food security in India. The effort is to identify those historical processes that are likely to have resulted in the marginalization of women from access and control over land. Selected historical evidence is explored and one such process is identified as a shift from communal ownership and access to natural resources, to increasing privatization and fragmentation of rights. Another is the increase in stratification and growth of hierarchies.

Why should women have rights to land? In the current discourse, this question has been posed in the narrow sense of women's individual ownership or title, but since women are firmly embedded within castes and classes, a rephrasing of the problematic is called for. The danger in focusing on individual rights in land for women is that it is likely to deflect from an emphasis on the redistribution of land to the landless. In the context of persistent landlessness, where the quantity of land to be redistributed remains miniscule, the demand of women for land rights is suggestive of sectarian interests, divisiveness within the family unit, and processes of fragmentation of holdings. The unstated assumption is that of women as a homogenous undifferentiated mass, rather like the term 'peasant' in the colonial literature. In fact posed in this way, the demand for women's rights to land skips many stages, ending up rather like a rhetorical device with a somewhat vague commitment towards women's empowerment, much like the slogan 'land to the tiller'. Unless the problem of landlessness per se is addressed, women's rights may serve to obfuscate the numerous layers of steps which need to be negotiated before gender equality in this sphere is likely to be achieved. It is argued here that the issue of women's rights to land has been narrowly defined precisely because of the incomplete nature of the process of land reforms.

However, to the extent that the issue of women's rights to land is seen as an enabling device for securing broad gender justice, it has and continues to play a significant role in articulating a demand along with a whole range of these, for say education or health, as guaranteed in the Constitution. It draws attention to women's invisibility in agriculture, the undervaluation of their economic contributions, the erosion of peasant women's roles and rights, and to a dominant ideology that encourages and endorses women's dependence within families, tendencies which have received a further fillip under the present phase of globalization. As early as 1979, the demand for land rights had already been articulated by Muslim peasant women at a Bengal conference where women identifying themselves as tillers, linked their future security to title in lands which were being redistributed by the government. The demand, which was incorporated into the Sixth Five Year Plan (Mazumdar 1997: 380) at the behest of representations made by several women's organizations, has since formed an important component of the women's rights discourse and is a significant goal of substantial sections of the women's movement. It is however the operational feasibility of the demand which remains problematic, given the glaring inequalities in the structure of landholdings, including landlessness and the persistence of feudal structures in large parts of the Indian state.

The emphasis on rights to land for women suggests a need to

redress the inequitable gender division of resources within households, and this draws attention to, and challenges, assumptions of gender equity within households. The problem of concretizing and realizing women's access to land may be approached in different ways. In one, where the focus is strictly on individual ownership rights and the concept of private property is central, women's ownership of land is envisaged as distinct and separate from that of men. In the second approach, favoured in the following pages, land and agriculture as the means of construction of new forms of social relations is envisaged, which also necessitates understanding the ways in which women have historically related to land. Insights from history inform the quest for pragmatic solutions to women's landlessness, such as joint and collective ownership and farming. A serious drawback of the first approach is its total reliance on the state to alter existing inequities in agrarian relations. This state-centric focus runs the risk of relying on yet another legislation or land reform, which may languish like many other well-intentioned legal initiatives in the past, particularly in the light of development initiatives of earlier decades wherein the understanding emerged that legislation without social empowerment of those for whom it is intended, is invariably meaningless. The second approach, on the other hand, addresses the problem of landlessness, by focusing on empowering the landless, and the effort is also to reaffirm and build on women's contributions in agriculture, thereby strengthening women's and grass-roots initiatives. To the extent that the latter approach also assumes state cooperation in making available some lands for collective farming, the onus of completing the hitherto unfinished process of land redistribution gets shifted to the state, in addition to ensuring that the state adhere to its land reform agenda at the local level.

While administrators have pointed out that there is simply not enough land for redistribution among the landless and in Bina Agarwal's estimation this amounts to not more than 0.56 per cent of the country's arable land, the shift in focus from individual to collective ownership affords a practical solution to the problem. In situations of extremely scarce resources, the emphasis on individual ownership has the dangerous potential of pitching one landless woman against another and thus promoting further divisiveness within an already divided social milieu.

A state-centric approach is also likely to view women in homogenized, oversimplified, monolithic, casteless terms. As women are embedded within caste, class and religious structures, it would be naïve to conceptualize a single formula for all categories of women. An intervention aimed at guaranteeing access to productive resources must be informed by the fact that a landless Dalit woman, owing to the layering of social and economc inequalities, is more severely disadvantaged and disempowered than a landless OBC or upper-caste woman. For instance if one were to enforce equal shares for sons and daughters in the ancestral landholdings, what meaning would this have for Dalits who have historically been landless?

For example according to a government estimate, there are only 605 acres of land to be redistributed in Jehanabad, Bihar; if distributed on an individual basis this would, at best, benefit barely 605 families. In contrast, in Nighwan village of the same district, 50 Dalit families survive on a mere 20 acres of collectively-owned land in addition to the fact that every worker gets more than minimum wages; a yearly bonus; seed for the next crop as well as savings for a common resource pool. The latter is used to finance the purchase of carpets, torches, lanterns, and utensils, i.e. items required for common use. A year ago, the community collectively built a stretch of road 2 km. in length, connecting the village to the main road. How land was obtained for road construction is an exemplary insight into the ingredients that make for successful collective initiatives: pieces of land were donated from individual holdings and landless Dalits donated labour time equivalent to land shares given by others (A. Kumar, personal communication, and field notes). This case illustrates the rich possibilities for community empowerment, including that of women, inherent in collective efforts, especially where the state may be dysfunctional. Had the land been divided among the 50 families, the division of the 20-acre pool would have resulted in unsustainable fragmented holdings, let alone providing savings for the development activities undertaken by the village community. The solution in fact precluded the extreme fragmentation that would have led to unviable holdings, underemployment and the need to seek employment outside the village.

Another reason to prioritize collective farming over the redistribution of land as individual holdings is illustrated by the

CWDS project in Bankura, which began in the village Jhilimili, West Bengal, in 1981. Women's mobilization here has resulted in a radical alteration of their status, along with respectability as path breakers in sustainable grass-roots organizations and leadership by poor peasant women. The reduction of dependence on seasonal migration for survival was combined with revival and expansion of the dying tassar industry, as well as introduction of other land-based productive activities through collective ownership and use of wastelands in the region. The demonstration effect of these women's groups was such that a federation of numerous women's collectives emerged in the area. Over the years, their activities have widened to include credit, vegetable cultivation, processing of minor forest produce, etc., while not relinquishing women's primary identity as specialists in agriculture and the management of natural resources.

Collective ownership is clearly empowering because of the sense of belonging it creates. It evokes an age-old historico-cultural memory because women have not owned land, they have always belonged to it. The current discourse on the other hand, is caught up in legal questions of who owns, who does not, etc. The discourse emerged after the forced transition from 'the earth' to land, a transition that changed belongingness to a commodity which could be measured, bought, mortgaged, sold, etc. To continue speaking in terms of legal discourse is to give up on the legacy of millennia. In this context, it may be worthwhile to reflect on the gender of land in regional languages, where *dharti* (land) evokes veneration as mother; or processes whereby terms such as *kisanin* for woman peasant have fallen into disuse over a period of time.

The case for women's empowerment through rights to land has been made most convincingly by Bina Agarwal in *A Field of One's Own* (1995). As the relationship between women and property has remained little theorized, her study has filled a much-needed gap. Agarwal covers a wide spectrum, pitching her work in the zone between development studies which treat the household as the analytical unit to the neglect of the intra-household gender dimension, and the sociological/anthropological literature wherein subordination is often linked to a society's given cultural values. Within the former, several assumptions common in development policy and economic theory have been predominant, such as gender congruence of interests within the family; employment and income generating schemes for the improvement of women's status; and land distribution leading to fragmentation and consequent reduction in agricultural productivity. Agarwal successfully challenges many of these assumptions. However, in exploring the ambiguities in public policy and law surrounding the question of women's rights to land, she takes issue with proponents of the class *vs* gender approach and positions herself firmly in favour of the latter.

This position leads Agarwal to emphasize the commonalities among women cutting across their derived class privileges/ deprivations, thus blurring class identification. Vulnerability to violence, responsibility for housework and childcare, gender inequalities in legal rights, risks arising from marital breakdown which may inflict destitution even on women of rich peasant households, etc., are cited as phenomena that cut across class lines. Thus the economic vulnerability of women is seen as contributing to the ambiguous character of their class position. These generalizations, while diluting an otherwise sound thesis, serve to dissociate women from their rootedness within the system of production, and attention is drawn away from the interlocking of class, caste and gender oppression.

The case for independent land rights for women is built on the basis of several arguments, particularly issues such as welfare (security against poverty); efficiency (access to credit, technology and institutional support which increase productivity); and equality and empowerment (enabling challenges to male oppression). According to the welfare argument, land rights for women would reduce the risk of female and household poverty largely because unlike men, women spend a majority of their earnings on the family's basic needs. Access to land also ensures women's access to credit, helping to increase production facilities and factors of production, which in turn ensures that high wages for agricultural labour are maintained, and the negotiation of better tenancy arrangements is possible. Control over land could encourage women to make long-term investments in land and increase their access to new technology and practices. All these factors would enhance the effectiveness of resource use and production. As observed by the Naugarh women, landownership would ensure better treatment from kin members particularly in the case of the elderly and widows. Finally, the empowerment argument enables women to challenge existing systems of subordination and the existing power relationships and enables resistance to violence.

The significance of analysing control over land rather than mere title to it is acknowledged, yet it is independent ownership and property rights, which are argued for. This also accounts for the weightage given to women's inheritance. As property, land is seen as providing women with a minimum measure of security in the face of marital discord, destitution and displacement, and this becomes the pivot on which hinges Agarwal's entire argument for women's land rights.

Hence in the final analysis, and perhaps implicitly, the landless get excluded from the picture. Further, Agarwal forgoes the option of delving into the 'contentious question of how women's subordination originated historically' (Agarwal 1995: 52), in favour of an exploration into the currently structured gender inequalities and the manner in which they are perpetuated. This avowed ahistoricism leads Agarwal to view land rights in the juridical sense alone, a choice that, further, has a bearing on the conclusions drawn and answers provided.

Agarwal's own data, representing a range of societies in varied stages of development and which have evolved through specific historical and cultural processes, dictate approaches to empowerment sensitive to these diversities. Consequently the demand for property rights in land will need to be negotiated within these complex agrarian structures and modified in accordance with them. For instance, how meaningful is it to speak of individual property rights for women in Garo society where land itself is communally owned and where men receive use rights in land according to familial needs and the number of family members? What form then is the struggle for women's empowerment to take here and should not the impetus for altered agrarian relations emerge from within society, particularly from women themselves? If empowerment lies in the process of struggle, the process may itself require alteration and redefinition in the light of the varied socio-cultural, economic and historical realities.

A rich body of literature from the field of anthropology on customary rights and associated practices has enabled cross-cultural comparisons as well as the possibility of postulating a link between women's property rights in land and certain marriage and residential customs which reduce the risk of land passing to non-kin. Anthropological literature has shown that wherever women in South Asia have customarily enjoyed rights in landed property, it has been associated with their residing in or having to reside within the natal village or even the natal home. This is worth contrasting with the evidence from north Indian patrilineal communities, where dowry-giving high castes such as Rajputs and Brahmins tend to have affinal links more distant from the natal village than do the lower caste groups without property.

Thus if affinal links are depicted as a series of concentric circles, spreading from the village outwards, high castes and property owning groups would have links farthest away from the core, at the widest possible distance from the centre, while the lower castes and landless would tend to marry within or close to the village. In Punjab, for instance, women's separation songs at marriage poignantly capture the bride's sense of displacement and propertyless status resulting from this spatial distance. It is noteworthy that it was precisely among landowning jats that women's customary inheritance had given way to the custom of *karewa*, i.e. marriage between a widow and her brother-in-law to ensure that widows would not claim their separate shares in the familial patrilineal property (Chowdhry 1995: 64-82).

A study of the comparative ethnographical material from a range of patrilineal, matrilineal and bilateral societies in South Asia shows that the stronger the practices of purdah and village exogamy, and the greater the spatial distance resulting from marriage, the higher are the chances of women giving up their claims to land. Agarwal draws these conclusions as well. In this context, the gap between the considerable legal rights to inherit landed property and the innumerable constraints that prevent women from actually exercising these rights is the subject of an interesting body of literature. In India while the constitutional guarantees in favour of women and progressive legislations are extremely gender-sensitive, a wide gap exists between theory and practice.

Despite the Hindu Succession Act of 1956, which grants equal inheritance rights to sons and daughters, or brothers and sisters, in patrilineal communities women only occasionally inherit as widows and extremely rarely as daughters. Prem Chowdhry, for instance, found in Haryana that rural society sees this enablement of females as a right to inherit two shares: as a daughter and as a widow, the dual inheritance being the evil that patriarchal forces have been determined to curb. However, the attack has been focused on the share of the daughter rather than that of the widow (1997: 289). Under this law, while widows are entitled to an absolute estate, rarely is this achieved in practice. Also, as tenancy rights in agricultural land are not covered by this law, there is a discrepancy between the devolution of agricultural land in several states and the inheritance laws. Even where existing legislations in theory grant equal shares to sons and daughters in the patrilineal property, it is very unlikely that daughters actually claim these shares. Patriarchal values have hitherto ensured that daughters rarely demand their share in the family property, on grounds that the voicing of such claims would drive a wedge between brothers and sisters or perceived as sisters' claims *against* their brothers.

The unease with daughters' rights of inheritance results in the activation of a set of social controls which include emphasis on notions of daughters as transitory members for whom shares in natal property cannot be allowed; the strengthening of brother-sister ties by ensuring that sisters relinquish their inheritance rights; legitimization of the use of force to prevent breaches of the above norms and prejudices and, finally, substitution of daughters' inheritance claims by dowry (ibid.: 291).The socialization of daughters further ensures that they themselves accept their exclusion. Women's main concern therefore is to establish themselves in the new family and acquire a status there; and dowry is looked upon as a necessary contribution towards this process. Moreover, realizing the increasing 'heavy expenditure' which marriage entails, women tend to view dowry, and not property, as their due (ibid.: 304). 'The only ideal and *izzatwala* (honourable) pattern of inheritance is acknowledged to be by males to males. This means basically that daughters and sisters who are potential introducers of fresh blood and new descent lines through their husbands are to be kept from exercising their inheritance rights' (Chowdhry 1997: 1025).

The following folksong from Bundelkhand, effectively captures the sentiment of sisters' prayers for the good health and prosperity of brothers, who will inherit the mantle of patriarchal households. In the face of this powerful ideology, wherein daughters accept the inherent inequalities without questioning their rights to inherit along with other claimants, it is easy to see why sisters rarely make claims to their rightful shares in the family property.

Deau to mai mori, Khurpi tiparia,
Tiparia are, duba khodan khon main jaon.
Veera! More Indra akhare kheliau .
Bau duba mori gaiyan jo khaihen
Khaihen are, be dehain gagar bhar doodh
Veera! More Indra akhare kheliau

Give me mother, a khurpi and a basket
I'm off to cut grass
My brother will wrestle (against the demons)
In the akhara of Indra.
The cows will eat the grass
And give a pitcher full of milk
My brother will wrestle (against the demons).

R.H. Mitra, 1969, *Bundelkhand ki Sanskriti aur Sahitya*,
Delhi: Rajkamal Prakashan (305)

Chowdhry points to the reinforcement of these sentiments which have received encouragement in the noticeable revival of the festival of Raksha Bandhan. She argues that the renewed sanctity it has claimed in north India can be traced to the enabling provisions of the Hindu Succession Act of 1956, which, in breaking away from the past, for the first time enabled daughter, sister, widow and mother to inherit property on equal terms with the son, including land, with full proprietary rights to its disposal (Chowdhry 1997: 1025). As a widow without heirs, a woman usually claims a share in her husband's patrilineal property as a limited estate, that is, only for her lifetime and with restrictions on alienation. Despite regional variations on this issue, restrictions seem to be continuing since colonial times. As discussed in a later chapter, colonial records from at least one district of UP early in this century reveal that in litigation involving women, the largest proportion is related to widows fighting for their claims against reversionary male heirs. A daughter was unlikely to inherit—rather, she held her father's property until her own son, who had been appointed to succeed to her father's property, in the absence of male collateral heirs, reached maturity.

Changes in Kerala's matrilineal system studied by Sardamoni provide rich insights into the rapid historical, economic and political transformation of communities. The changes set in motion by colonial legislations early in this century regarding inheritance, succession, marriage and joint family vastly altered the matrilineal system. Significantly, the reforms themselves initiated by a male elite, struck at the roots of women's security and enabled male *karanavans* or property managers to appropriate for themselves far greater powers than ever before. According to Sardamoni, this appears to have been the logical conclusion to a process begun as early as 1912, when archival and anthropological sources indicate that the senior-most woman head of the *taravad* was being replaced by the eldest male as the *karnavan*, a trend which was institutionalized only after the establishment of British rule (Saradamoni 1996: 133-54).

Traditional organizational structures of communities with clear recognition of women's rights in land can serve as models of alternative institutional arrangements for landownership and use, when promoting land rights today. While this may smack of nostalgia for the past, it is significant to recall Gerda Lerner's cautionary remarks in this context: 'abandoning the search for an empowering past—the search for matriarchy—is the first step in the right direction. The creation of compensatory myths of the distant past for women will not emancipate women in the present and future' (Lerner 1986: 36). Lerner suggests, instead, conceptualizing women's roles in history, thereby creating a consciousness which can liberate women now.

PATTERNS OF LANDHOLDING IN UTTAR PRADESH

The pattern of landownership in Uttar Pradesh, despite being highly uneven, is such that a relatively small proportion of the population is entirely landless. Compared to other major states, UP has the second lowest proportion of agricultural labourers in the rural male labour force. On the other hand, it has the second-highest proportion of rural male workers reporting cultivation as their primary occupation. This has contributed to the predominance of interests of prosperous farmers in rural politics and also accounts for the small proportion of class-based mobilization aimed at radical agrarian reform in contrast to West Bengal and Kerala, where mobilization along class lines has led to far-reaching agrarian reforms and changes concerning participatory democracy.

Understandably the farmers' movements are hostile to demands relating to wage labour, women's emancipation and economic equality. A great gulf exists between landowning middle castes such as Jats and Yadavs and the untouchable Chamars, which is reflected in the hostility of farmers' movements to the interests of the Scheduled Castes and agricultural labourers (Dreźe and Gazdar 1998: 102).

The coincidence of political power and ritual authority and hence the mutually reinforcing functions of caste, class and gender inequalities account for the great resilience and persistence of these inequalities in UP, and an environment which is inhospitable to social change or broad-based political participation. These factors also constrain the scope for collaborative public action. Being

TABLE 1: PERCENTAGE DISTRIBUTION OF HOUSEHOLDS OVER FIVE BROAD CLASSES (1992, 1982 AND 1971-2)

	Year	*Marginal holdings*	*Small medium holdings*	*Semi-holdings*	*Medium holdings*	*Large holdings*	*All holdings*
All India	1992	71.88	13.42	9.28	4.54	0.88	100.00
	1982	66.64	14.07	10.78	6.45	1.42	100.00
	1971-2	62.62	15.49	11.94	7.83	2.12	100.00
UP	1992	74.40	14.73	7.92	2.76	0.21	100.00
	1982	67.95	17.38	10.23	4.06	0.37	100.00
	1971-2	65.58	18.60	10.84	4.49	0.49	100.00

Source: *Sarvekshana*, October-December 1995, p. 66.

TABLE 2: PERCENTAGE DISTRIBUTION OF AREA OWNED OVER FIVE BROAD CLASSES (1992, 1982 AND 1971-2)

	Year	*Marginal holdings*	*Small medium holdings*	*Semi-holdings*	*Medium holdings*	*Large holdings*	*All holdings*
All India	1992	16.93	18.59	24.58	26.07	13.83	100.00
	1982	12.22	16.49	23.58	29.83	18.07	100.00
	1971-2	9.76	14.68	21.92	30.73	22.91	100.00
UP	1992	27.42	24.88	25.82	18.14	3.73	100.00
	1982	20.36	24.08	28.11	22.25	5.18	100.00
	1971-2	17.49	24.65	27.94	23.85	6.07	100.00

Source: *Sarvekshana*, October-December 1995, p. 66.

TABLE 3: AVERAGE SIZE OF HOUSEHOLD OWNERSHIP HOLDINGS (RURAL)

	Average area owned per household (0.00 ha.)	*% of landless households*	*Average area owned per household owning land (ha.)*
All India	1.01	11.3	1.14
Uttar Pradesh	0.83	4.9	0.87

Source: *Sarvekshana*, October-December 1995, p. 63.

TABLE 4: PERCENTAGE OF LANDLESS AND SEMI-LANDLESS HOUSEHOLDS

	% of landless households			*% of landless & semi-landless households*		
	1971-2	*1982*	*1992*	*1971-2*	*1982*	*1992*
All India	9.6	11.3	11.3	37.4	39.9	42.4
Uttar Pradesh	4.6	4.9	4.9	32.7	30.9	34.6

Source: *Sarvekshana*, October-December 1995, p. 67.

Marginal holdings	less than 1.01 ha.
Small holdings	1.01 to 2.00 ha.
Medium holdings	4.01 to 10.00 ha.
Large holdings	larger than 10.00 ha.

steeped in traditional inequalities makes it harder for the underclasses to challenge caste, class and gender oppression.

Several studies have pointed to the tendency of Uttar Pradesh to lag behind the rest of the country in several significant aspects of social progress. The persistence of endemic deprivation and high levels of mortality, fertility, morbidity, undernutrition, illiteracy, social inequality, a slow pace of poverty decline and the lack of women's agency have been cited as the most notable features contributing to underdevelopment in the state (Dreze and Gazdar 1998: 33). Soon after Independence, within the official goals of public policy, social and economic development became primary and the Zamindari Abolition Act succeeded in eliminating feudal intermediaries, leading to the redistribution of proprietary rights in land among a vast majority of landless tenant farmers, but the democratization of society did not go much further.

CHAPTER OUTLINE

Following the initial discussion of the points of departure and main themes of the book, successive chapters are organized with a focus on particular classes of rural women within given social formations, i.e. distinct geographical locations and delimited time-spans. Questions about women and land and the impact of historical processes are separately examined by focusing in turn on the women of landowning groups, peasant women, landless women and those most marginalized in the agrarian structure. Though each chapter tells a different story from a distinct vantage point, the narration of the movement from colonial to recent society in Uttar Pradesh, aims at generalizing from the specifics (which are selective and chosen particularly for the light they throw on the processes one is concerned with). The chapters offer distinct case material and evidence, which allows for the detailed construction of women and their access to land, and the complexities thereof, in Uttar Pradesh through the past century.

In the first chapter the points of departure for this work are set out. It explores theories of women's subordination, particularly the opposition between biological and historical theories; between those which see the sexual division of labour as natural and those which see it as linked to woman's participation in productive activity and their access to productive resources. Recent anthropological research on this theme is discussed. The chapter then goes on to develop some hypotheses relating to historical processes whereby women lose access to productive resources and land. The first process analysed as the shift from communal to private ownership of the means of production, draws on anthropological and ethnographical insights of a secondary nature, supplemented by relevant historical evidence from ancient India. The second section analyses the growth of agriculture and the processes of differentiation within society, including reasons for the increasing undervaluation of manual labour. The third contour analyses Sanskritization and women in the processes of upward mobility, largely during the course of the twentieth century. The analysis of the manner in which distinct caste identities were sought to be shaped through a focus on the role of their women, draws, among other sources, on the caste pamphlet literature published during this century.

The next chapter presents a concrete exploration of one of the hypotheses set out in the previous chapter, i.e. the utilization of women's labour in the increasing differentiation within society providing the impetus for the processes of surplus accumulation and economic and social transformation. This chapter is an exercise in understanding peasant differentiation through a re-reading of historical evidence from Faizabad district of colonial Awadh. The focus on women's roles in agrarian production attempts to redress the overwhelming male bias in agrarian studies where assumptions of gender neutrality have rendered women invisible. Within the literature, the depictions of the peasant as male and the peasantry as undifferentiated and homogenous have obscured class and gender differentiations. The chapter argues that if access to and control over productive resources as well as productive skills of peasant women are factored into the analysis, the differentiation within the peasantry becomes clearer. It investigates the role of the utilization of women's productivity in the increasing differentiation between classes.

Chapter 2 also explores the interlinkages between caste, class and gender in an effort to comprehend the institutions and practices within which peasant women's lives were embedded. The review of agricultural operations in the countryside dependent on women's labour puts into perspective the complex contributions of women of peasant castes in the countryside. These belonged largely to the castes of Kachi, Kurmi and Koeri, recognized today as the Other Backward Classes (OBCs). An attempt is made to analyse how the traditions of a caste and its position within the caste hierarchy determine the extent to which women's labour within the household can be enlisted for production. The extent to which the state tacitly accepts and endorses caste customs is seen in the light of the colonial state's political and economic calculations. This forms the entry point for more exhaustive explorations of the role of the state to be analysed in later chapters. The emphasis in this chapter makes a small beginning towards a more holistic analysis of socio-historical processes.

In Chapter 3 is explored the colonial state's intervention in the form of concrete legislation with far-reaching implications for class and gender. The focus is now on a small and exclusive, politically influential class of proprietary landholders, i.e. the taluqdars of Awadh, who were viewed by the colonial state as the bulwark of

British rule in the province. In examining the intended and unintended consequences of the Taluqdari Succession Act of 1869, I explore processes whereby the status of taluqdari women (both Hindu and Muslim) deteriorated owing to continued disabilites and exclusion from ownership and control of taluqas despite their belonging to the class of landholders. Thus the kinds of spaces that were available for taluqdari women, as well as the disadvantages spelt by the Act, such as loss of flexibility of customs and harsher controls, and restrictions vis-à-vis their male relatives, are some of the threads running through the chapter which also allow for explorations of continuities and ruptures with traditions. A number of Awadh court cases and histories of taluqas provide the source material for this enquiry. The concern is to push forward one's understanding of women and land—in this case women of the landowning class, the majority of whom, in Awadh, were of the Rajput or Kshatriya caste.

Chapters 4 and 5, based on fieldwork in two distinct areas of UP, a village in Varanasi district and a village cluster in Manikpur, Banda, explore contemporary problems of landlessness and the processes of marginalization of women on the lowest rungs of the caste and class hierarchies. The study of Sarai Mohana on the banks of the Ganga is framed by a discussion which interrogates the role of the state in constituting and sustaining the structures of subordination arising from differential ownership and control. I have used secondary sources to investigate the Mughal and Peshwa states and construct arguments about the institutionalization of gender inequalities and patriarchies, and the roles of different states in sustaining and constituting them. Conclusions about the nature of the state are then applied to the case study of a village largely inhabited by the Mallah caste traditionally involved in boating and fishing, which has been facing marginalization and a systematic erosion of livelihood over a fifty-year period. Issues confronting the community are linked to the Land Alienation Act of 1894, under which the village commons were made over to a private foundation for educational purposes. The story of Sarai Mohana is one of peoples' struggles against the state and the role of women in these struggles.

The final chapter pushes further the investigations on the problematic of marginalization of women from land and other productive resources, this time at the micro-level and within the context of land reforms and land redistribution drives in UP. One hears tales of women's pathos and struggles for survival in a milieu where the state has abdicated its responsibility and commitment to gender justice, and where alienation from land and forest constitutes their experience. With the focus on landless Kol tribal women of Banda district, who do not receive state recognition as Scheduled Tribes, a new look at land reforms from the point of view of the women is presented. The problems encountered by women in the processes involving the distribution of land to the landless, forms the central theme of this chapter. The enquiry explores the centrality of women's access and control over land and productive resources, where the very survival of families and entire communities is dependent on the women.

contexts of land reforms and land redistribution drives in UP. One hears tales of women's pathos and struggles for survival in a milieu where the state has abdicated its responsibility and commitment to gender justice, and where alienation from land and forest constitutes their experience. With the focus on landless Kol tribal women of Banda district, who do not receive state recognition as Scheduled Tribes, a new look at land reforms from the point of view of the women is presented. The problems encountered by women in the processes involving the distribution of land to the landless forms the central theme of this chapter. The enquiry explores the centrality of women's access and control over land and productive resources, where the very survival of families and entire communities is dependent on the women.

CHAPTER 1

Land, Caste and Gender: Some Hypotheses

I'll grow my hair long as a falling river.
When I die that's all I'll take with me.

No authority and no property.
Even newly hatched chickens claw at her.

Reflections by members of Stri Shakti Mandal, an organization of poor peasant women near Pune, cited in G. Poitevin and H. Rairkar, 1993, *Indian Peasant Women Speak Up*, Bombay: Orient Longman (79, 140)

The denial of property rights to women is a significant instrument of patriarchy, especially if one sees patriarchy as a 'historically developed cultural ideological force, giving gender relations their specific character in each situation' (Banerjee 1995: 142).[1] Patriarchy thus understood leads to an exploration of processes by which gender is constructed and the role played by patriarchy in those processes. The social construction of gender needs to be studied historically in order to isolate the manner in which inequitable distribution of power, authority and resources has occurred in history with the systematic underprivileging of women in different social formations. A focus on women's access to land leads us into questions relating to the emergence of patriarchy, class divisions and the state. However, the aim of the present chapter is limited to identifying the historical processes whereby women have lost access and control over land and productive resources. A fallout of the present enquiry will include insights into the extent to which suppression of women has played a role in the formation of caste society and in maintaining separation between castes through features such as endogamy. The chapter is divided into four sections relating (1) to anthropological insights on questions of women's access and control over resources, followed by a discussion on (2) women's roles in production, (3) the growth of hierarchies and their implications for gender relations, and (4) an analysis of more concrete evidence pertaining to the efforts of various caste groups for upward mobility during the course of this century. A theme running through this chapter is the devaluation of 'manual' labour and its implications for women's roles in production.

The evidence of women's involvement in agriculture has increasingly challenged biological theories of women's subordination, particularly those that have treated the opposition between men and women as fundamental and universal. The fact that women's efforts led to the domestication of plants and the invention of agriculture, however, remain obscured by both current and historical discourses which have systematically treated the peasant as male, raising further questions about women's marginalization within the power and resource systems that govern agriculture. In anthropological writings, the inability to explain why one set of activities carried out by males should be more highly valued and lead to greater social power, stems from a treatment of women as passive participants, commodities in a universe created by men and valued largely for their reproductive capacities which prevents them from achieving status as producers (Evans-Pritchard 1965; Levi-Strauss 1968; Meillassoux 1981). In the 1980s, Leacock and Etienne questioned such views that not only determined the conceptual framework of anthropology but also the selection and organization of data (Leacock and Etienne 1980). The political and ideological structures that have developed which subordinate women may then be probed, allowing for the identification of processes whereby women's subordination is likely to have occurred. The historical evidence marshalled here is largely illustrative of the nature of these processes.

Here the focus is on two major and inter-related areas of change which I hypothesize as having determined and directly affected women's access to land. First, in the course of the shift from communal ownership and access to natural resources to increasing privatization and fragmentation of rights, women are increasingly divorced from access and control. The second shift may be identified as increasing social stratification and the growth of inequalities that rest on the undervaluation of manual labour and the consequent extension of this to the undervaluation of all peasant women's labour. As a corollary to the above, social norms and/or

Sanskritization processes wherein women's non-participation in visible labour is indicative of a family or caste's high status—a feature which has received continuous reinforcement from upwardly mobile groups. The relevance of understanding these processes acquires greater magnitude in the light of further reinforcement, not only under colonialism but also under current thrusts towards globalization. Historically these processes appear to have been at work to cause shifts in the ability of women not only to participate and contribute towards production, but also in their capacity to own or have access to valued productive resources. The emphasis on these processes facilitates the identification of the distinct advantages or deprivations suffered by different classes of women in different social structures. In addition, the role of ideological factors in strengthening and perpetuating the subordination of women may be probed. Needless to say, women of different castes would have differential access to land.

That high status in the caste hierarchy was usually a function of ownership and control over resources, mainly land, is commonplace. Land was also a source of extra-economic power in agrarian systems. However, ownership and control over productive resources did not mean the same thing for both men and women of the upwardly mobile caste groups. While it meant enhanced status and power for the men, it often meant greater and stricter controls over the women. One rarely hears of women owning and controlling land as the means of production. While some may have enjoyed certain economic and cultural gains as a consequence of the economic affluence of their caste, such as themselves not participating in labour, this meant access to a certain level of luxury denied to women of labouring castes. However, in highly stratified societies and those in which notions of hierarchy are well developed, women appear to be disadvantaged in certain ways.

Thus in probing the question of what value women as opposed to men attach to land, it may be found that instead of land rights merely constituting control over a piece of property, its meaning for rural women would stretch to include a range of socio-cultural and economic possibilities such as security against poverty, status, capacity to challenge societal and domestic violence and oppression, greater control over intra-household distribution of resources, access to credit, information and technology, and also a sense of identity, rootedness and belonging (Agarwal 1994: 1-40). Land and property relations including associated legal and ideological practices have different meanings for women. As recent studies increasingly show, the issue of property and land rights is gendered and is indicative of the balance of power not merely between classes but also between genders (Rao and Rana 1997: 1308).

WOMEN'S SUBORDINATION AND PRODUCTIVE RESOURCES

Anthropological Insights

Anthropologists have enquired into the roots of women's subordination cross-culturally. During the 1970s, efforts to establish women's agency in society were reflected in studies dealing with the extent and nature of women's subordination (Boserup 1970; Tinker 1990). The main question is the universal subordination of women and the explanatory frameworks that have been generated.

Karen Sacks in her analysis of six African societies makes a typology of three pre-class modes of production. In the first, the Communal Mode among the hunting gathering Mbuti, there are no classes and no centralized authority. Women share economic and political power with men. In the second type, the 'Kin Corporate Mode' among the Lovedu, it is kin groups which hold property and organize production. Sacks' thesis is that as one moves up the evolutionary scale, one finds that women lose some of their control over production and become dependent on husbands to a variable extent for life's necessities. Sacks goes on to show that when women stay on in the village of origin, they enjoy ownership over the means of production with brothers, but where they move to the husband's village, they occupy subordinate positions as wives. As women lose their social, economic and political privileges in society, one sees submissive behaviour, restrictions, and hard work becoming obligatory for women living in the husband's clan (Sacks 1979). Among the Kusasi of north-eastern Ghana, for instance, women are 'married in' from other communities and hence do not receive land in their own right, though they may enjoy use rights through husbands or other male kinsmen. They are deprived of not only independent access to land, but also command over the labour of their 'social superiors' and allocation of surplus produce. Here men enjoy a dominant role in determining women's access to land (Whitehead 1985: 176-92).

Engels presents an evolutionary account by which women are transformed from free and equal productive members of society to subordinate dependent wives and wards. He points out that the cause of transformation lies in the growth of male-oriented private property within the family, which appropriates and perpetuates it (Sacks 1979: 108). Under communal ownership of productive resources by the tribe or clan and production for use to meet subsistence needs, both productive work of men and household work were of equal significance. A shift occurred when membership in the clan no longer depended on the performance of public or social labour. The material base for women's transformation from being equal members of society to subordinate wives lies in the development of valuable productive resources, initially the domestication of large animals as private property. The latter became possible only when technical development and natural resources allowed a society to develop the skills needed to domesticate animals or invest labour in land so that its productivity lasted for a length of time.

As property became privately owned, smaller family units shattered the communal political economy of the clans, transforming gender relations within households. As production for exchange eclipsed production for use, the nature of the households, the significance of women's work within it and consequently women's position—all were transformed, women now worked for husbands and families instead of society (Sacks 1979).

It has been argued that women may be important, powerful and influential but relative to men of their age and status, women everywhere lack culturally valued authority and that cultural systems give greater authority and value to the roles and activities of men (Rosaldo and Lamphere 1974: 1-9). Women's status was found to be lowest in those societies where there is a firm differentiation between domestic and public spheres of activity and where women are isolated from one another and placed under a single man's authority in the home (ibid.). Sanday finds that women's status is highest in those societies where their contribution to subsistence is relatively equivalent to that of men. There women tend to control crucial economic resources. This in turn would lead to either antagonism between the sexes or to recognition of women in ritual and religious spheres (ibid.: 12). Sacks suggests that it is control of production rather than the amount of foodstuffs produced by women that determines women's status (ibid.). On the other hand, egalitarianism appears to be a feature of societies where the public and domestic sphere are only weakly differentiated, where neither sex claims much authority and the focus of social life is the home (ibid.: 36). Evidence suggests that some band societies are egalitarian, in the sense of individuals having autonomy, but current usages of concepts derived from societies with power, hierarchy and property may actually distort the understanding of social evolution. In egalitarian forms there may be no distinction between public and private spheres and there is generalized sharing based on open access to all basic resources. The division of labour by sex binds the sexes in reciprocal exchange relations without female dependence on males in individual families (Leacock 1986: 107-35). Studies have shown that there is a complex of processes involved, which moves societies towards class differentiation so that specialization, exchange and expenditure of labour on land all contribute towards class differentiation.

Ethnographic evidence of foragers shows that women exercise considerable control over their lives in such societies where there is no differential access to resources through private ownership and no specialization of labour beyond that by sex, nor market systems to intervene in direct relationships between production and distribution. 'Unless some form of control over resources enables persons with authority to withhold them from others, authority is not authority as we know it'(ibid. 1978: 249). Here dispersal of authority meant that the private-public and jural-familial dichotomy so important in hierarchically organized societies was not relevant and, among the Iroquois for instance, even household management had a public character.

Further, the range of decisions made by women among the Ojibwa, for instance, make apparent women's autonomous and public roles. Men are assigned the task of hunting and securing raw materials while women are expected to manufacture out of the raw material. There is a relation between status and the ability to control the conditions of work and distribution of goods produced. In these societies, women may not have been literal equals of men but they had their own rights, duties and responsibilities which were complementary and in no way secondary to those of men. The essence seems to lie in whether or not women control the conditions of this work and the dispensation of the goods they produce (ibid. 1978: 252). Hence in egalitarian societies, while women are limited by the same technological and ecological considerations that men are, there is no socially defined group that directs their activities (ibid. 1978: 252).

Leacock emphasizes that though divisions based on sex are a human universal, they need not entail sexual hierarchy. Further, differences in function need not imply social inequalities and that where inequalities exist, they are the consequence of the differential control of resources and distribution of basic necessities (ibid. 1978: 265). In outlining the mechanisms that transformed egalitarian structures into family-based entreprenurial ones, it was seen that from the collective economy, the family emerged and took shape as an economic unit that transformed women's work from public production to private household service.

> The critical development that triggered the change was the specialization of labour that increasingly replaced production of goods for use by production of commodities for exchange and set up economic relationships that lay beyond the control of producers. The complex of processes involved, concerned specialization, exchange and the expenditure of labour on land, together with initial steps towards class differentiation. (ibid.)

Leacock's critics have however pointed out that if a distinction is made between power and authority wherein the latter includes the right to allocate resources, then one finds that men had greater authority in band societies. This is also reflected in the fact that leadership of organized activity involving both sexes was in the male domain. Finally, to substitute 'pre-class' for 'band' societies appears to suggest a simple unilinear evolutionism. However, by posing the question as what are a society's cultural values and what processes organize the distribution of prestige, power and privilege, it may be possible to arrive at a greater understanding of how inequality is organized in distinct societies (Collier and Yanagisako 1987: 40).

Anthropologists like Morton Klass have suggested that with the beginning of food production in favourable ecological zones, after the hunting and gathering stage and domestication of plants and animals, absolute surpluses became available with new technologies, which favoured those corporate groups that had possession of lands. A hierarchy of corporate groups developed, owing to unequal access to control of economic resources leading to the transition from clan to caste. Klass has emphasized differential access to basic resources and economic inequality of corporate groups in the emergence of the caste system (Klass 1998: 180-6).

TRANSFORMATION IN GENDER RELATIONS IN INDIA

COMMUNAL TO PRIVATE OWNERSHIP OF LAND

Many processes and tendencies observed by anthropologists are in evidence in India even today, allowing for analysis of current transformations in gender relations. The tribal evidence is abundantly illustrative of the hypothesis about the negative implications for women's access to productive resources with the shift from communal to private ownership of the means of production. As in the ethnographic accounts of band societies discussed above, where a rigidly defined division of labour by sex may be lacking, it is seen that the Birhor of Jharkhand display features of communal forms as they are hunter-gatherers organized in bands. While there is a division of labour which separates women's work from that of men, no strong taboos exist to prevent men and women from undertaking each other's productive tasks (Nathan 1997: 247), especially in the spheres of rope-making, hunting and house construction. Hunting in the deep forests is, however, taboo for women. As women were prominent in the sale and barter of rope, their involvement in exchanges with the outside world had a public character which was almost as much if not more important than men's public activities. Men's prominent public activities concerned decision-making about band affairs such as moving from location to location and involvement in the ritual and magico-religious spheres. Hence, while men produced the prestige goods, controlled the rituals and represented the community, the informal authority wielded by them was offset by women's control of regular economic exchanges.

Further, while patriclocality is the preferred form of residence, both matri- and patri-local residence exist, brothers and sisters tending to move together after marriage, suggesting the mutual exchange of sisters and daughters. The flexibility in residence patterns suggests that not just women but men are also exchanged.

The emphasis on sharing, the primacy of group interests, band members being related by ties of blood or marriage and the absence of any accumulation of goods or individual property make for a balance in gender relations. Above all, access to productive resources was not monopolized by any particular group since in band society residence gives rights to the use of resources.

Another tribe which appears to exhibit relative equality in gender relations is the Jatapu of Andhra Pradesh, practising swidden agriculture, characterized by complementarity in productive activity between the sexes and joint labour by women and men, none of the tasks being privileged over others as in plough agriculture (ibid.: 251). Here, men clear the trees and burn them while women cultivate the swidden fields as well as manage the produce. In swidden agriculture, the absence of a settled village community as well as the need for shifting habitation results in land itself being viewed as communal property. However, what happens to land when slash and burn agriculture become part of a settled village system may be seen in the case of the Khasis of Meghalaya. Here while property is inherited in the female line, managerial and extra-family representation is the domain of men. Gradually the sphere of rituals, the domain of men, acquires greater importance than the sphere of production, comprising the technical knowledge controlled by women, as the product of labour begins to be seen as crucially dependent on the performance of rituals (ibid.: 253). Men's attempts to establish their own authority in the ritual and magico-religious sphere and exclude the women from it, result in bitter struggles and resistance by women as seen in the Santhal history of witches and witch hunting (ibid.: 254).

Hence, 'the denunciation of ritual knowledge by women as evil, can be seen as an attempt by the denouncers (men) to change the established order (which very likely was one of joint authority of men and women) and to set up in its place an order based on the sole authority of men' (ibid.: 255). In this manner the shared authority of the sexes in the swidden and gathering economies, which were also largely bilateral, was sought to be changed into the sole authority of men in plough agriculture with patrilineal descent. Witch hunting, a common occurrence among the Santhals (but by no means exclusively among them) even today is directed usually at widows, which results in lands passing to the husbands' male agnates, the destruction of the widows' life interest in the lands being the economic objective, which in turn reflects the larger struggle to establish the rights of the patrilineage to agricultural land. As Jaiswal (1998: 9) has pointed out, the establishment of patrilocality and clan exogamy would no doubt have resulted in strengthening patriarchal trends and the increasing subordination of women. Patriarchy therefore becomes intrinsic to the process of stratification.

In communal tenure with individual possession as among the Santhals, women had definite rights in land. As widows, women have the right to maintenance from the land as well as to supervise cultivation and manage the land. However, with the growth of individual tenure it is possible to see how women's land rights are eroded from an earlier life interest, to a right to maintenance and then to living at the mercy of male relatives. With the establishment of full-fledged patriarchy, fathers, husbands or sons mediate women's relations with land. In some tribes such as the Santhal, Munda and Ho, community forms of landownership still exist. In these economies, gathering plays a significant part in the domestic economy and women continue to have control over sales from the forest produce (ibid.: 271).

The folklore and temple murals of some tribes suggest that women had always played a significant role in agriculture. In communities practising *jhum* or shifting cultivation, agriculture still remains a monopoly of women. According to M.S. Swaminathan, rice agriculture was the discovery of women in South and South-East Asia. He attributes the continuation of some highly specialized skills among certain tribal women, such as hand pollination, to their use by generations of female agricultural specialists (Swaminathan 1985).

Clearly the evidence points to a fair degree of gender equality within foraging and hunting-gathering tribes. However, as these tribes are incorporated into wider societies, there is erosion of egalitarian tendencies and the growth of restrictions on women. These conclusions are substantiated by studies on tribal formations in medieval Punjab where 'an almost imperceptible process towards sedentarization of those which were nomadic and to a great stratification amongst those which had already sedentarised' has been noted (Singh 1988: 325). More recently it appears that throughout South-West Asia nomadic people became tied in relations of dependence and reciprocity to sedentary communities in the area (ibid.: 332). Further, 'so close a relationship did tribal pastoralism bear with the sedentary and commercialized agrarian society of Mughal Punjab, and so inextricably linked were its economic interests with those of the latter, that fundamental shifts in the structure of any one of these societies could hardly have left the other unaffected' (ibid.: 340). Nathan concludes,

> when a hunter-gatherer tribe settled down and became agricultural labourers, they carried on much of their earlier gender practices. On the other hand, when an agriculturist-gatherer tribe settled down as landowning agriculturists, they tended to change the earlier gender practices, and adopt those characteristics of caste Hinduism. The differences in gender practices were then themselves identified as marks of caste rank. (Nathan 1997: 271)

Shifting from anthropological to historical evidence, it is seen that in recognition of the economic role of women, many prehistoric societies appear to have been matrilineal. Gordon Childe suggests that among pure cultivators owing to the role of the women's contributions to the collective economy, kinship is naturally reckoned in the female line and the system of mother-right prevails. With stockbreeding, on the contrary, economic and social influence pass to the males and kinship is patrilineal (Childe 1976: 73), a view which perhaps owes to that of Engels. In this context Gerda Lerner's warning about the futility of the search for matriarchy as an alternative empowering past in the quest for disproving the universal subordination of women and thus providing compensatory myths of the distant past, particularly in the absence of adequate or conclusive historical or archaeological evidence, is pertinent (Lerner 1986: 36). The Indian evidence from cultural myths and folklore does, however, point to the submergence of matriarchal traditions by patriarchal ones. Kosambi has drawn attention to the widespread prevalence of female deities and cults in rural India, which may be attributed to the predominance of matriarchal communities in the past. The increasing dominance of the Aryans over the original peoples of the subcontinent sometimes submerged these traditions altogether and occasionally assimilated them within the mainstream cultural traditions.

> Matriarchal elements had been won over by identifying the mother goddess with the wife of some male god. The complex divine household carried on the process of syncretism. . . . The marriage of the gods imply human

> marriages as a recognised institution, and would be impossible without social fusion of their formerly separate and even inimical devotees. The resultant social combination was more productive, with a better mastery of the environment. (Kosambi 1975: 11)

In this way, it appears that fairly contradictory ideologies coexisted through the process of assimilation of cultural myths. In many significant areas of social life relating to learning, wealth generation, energy, change and survival against destructive forces, the influence of matriarchal symbols finds expression even today.

The local pre-Aryan indigenous population appears to have observed mother right, especially at the stage where there was no concept of private property. Thus the first clans were matriarchal, while fathers were often not recognized even as having any procreative function (Kosambi 1975). In the Vedic age, the Vedic tribes were known as Jana and others were called Janya. The latter were given a place in coronation rituals, whereby relations between the two groups were cemented (Sharma 1983: 22). The fact that four out of about a dozen *ratnins*[2] to whose house the king went in connection with a coronation ritual were women, shows that due concessions were made to matriarchal customs of the Vedic tribes (Kosambi 1975). Indeed matriarchal customs still survive in those parts of the country that took last to plough agriculture, as in Travancore, Cochin. The change to male dominance appears to have occurred when the holding of special property by males developed. In general, this meant cattle, which were first herded for meat, later for milk products and skins and finally used as a source of power in agriculture and transport. Thus patriarchy, individual property and class divisions appear to have become possible though not always inevitable.

In this context what Karve has to say is of significance:

> Little is known about historical struggles which took place before the productivity of men's relation to nature could establish itself as superior to that of women. But from ideological battles described in ancient Indian literature that went on for several centuries over the question of whether nature of product (grain, children) was determined by field (woman) or by seed (man) we can assume that the subordination of female productivity was by no means a peaceful process but part and parcel of class struggles and the establishment of patriarchal property relations over land, cattle and women. (Karve 1964 cited in Mies 1988: 78)

Developing this line of argument further, Mies argues that men could develop productivity independent of women's only on the basis of developed female productivity. Female productivity consisted above all in the ability to provide daily subsistence. Hence the survival of human populations has been due much more to woman the gatherer than man the hunter (ibid. 1988: 78-9).

The productive forces of the hunters could be fully released only at the stage when pastoral nomads, who domesticated cattle and women, invaded agricultural communities. This means the full realization of the productive capacity of the predatory mode of production presupposes the existence of other really productive modes like agriculture. According to Elizabeth Fisher, the breeding of animals through coercion, with the object of increasing herds, was the beginning of dominance over women. As this logic gets extended, women become part of moveable property like cattle. Fisher has shown that for pastoral nomads, women were no longer very important as producers and gatherers of food, as was the case among hunters. They were needed as breeders of children, especially sons. Their productivity was then reduced to fertility, to be appropriated and controlled by men (Fisher 1979: 248). Further, the unequal division of labour by sex, once established by means of violence, was then upheld by means of institutions like family and state and also by means of powerful ideological systems.

Growth of Agriculture and Processes of Differentiation

The advent of agriculture and its growth in ancient India, especially the control over land, was organized along caste lines in which the upper strata had control over land, while the lower strata had to work on it. It is important to study the linkages between evolution of the caste system, social relations of agrarian production and the state as the social and cultural arbiter without any claim to autonomy. Jaiswal links the evolution of the caste system to the emergence of patriarchy, class divisions and the state. She argues that occupational specialization and hierarchical gradation went hand in hand with the suppression of women and all these together play a crucial role in the formation of caste society as well as in regulating its internal relationships (Jaiswal 1998: 6). How exactly the growth of social differentiation resulted in the emergence of the caste system (in order to institutionalize differentiation) is a question of great historical importance. However, the purpose is to trace women's position as differentiation became increasingly marked among the agriculturists.

While social anthropologists have outlined three fundamental characteristics of caste organization as hierarchy, inherited occupational specialization and endogamy, it is the latter which has been cited as the feature which contributed to the regulation and reproduction of patriarchy and the hierarchy of social groups, and, in the process, acquired rigidity. Jaiswal points out that what scholars have ignored is the role of patriarchy and subjugation of women in the ideology and rules of endogamy (ibid.). An important and connected question relates to the persistence of endogamy even when other caste characteristics such as occupation and hierarchy have disappeared—a question I shall address in a later section of this chapter.

The Undervaluation of Manual Labour

Also interesting in the anthropological literature is concern with the processes by which women's work gets devalued. The concept of the sexual division of labour conceals the fact of men's tasks being usually considered as cultural (conscious, rational, planned and innately productive) whereas women's tasks are seen as determined by their nature (emotional, nurturing and caring). Anthropologists have not only asked when the division of labour arose between men and women, but also how this division of labour became a relationship of dominance and exploitation, why it became asymmetric and hierarchical. It has been pointed out that women developed the first truly productive relationship with nature. With the invention of plant cultivation, it became possible to conceive for the first time of a productive society (after the gathering stage). Women not only collected and consumed what grew in nature but also made things grow, giving rise to social production and sharing, the first social relation being between mothers and children (Mies 1988: 76).

In the historical literature it is possible to posit a connection between the growth of the Shudra varna and the undervaluation of all labour, which is then extended to include the labour of women of both upper and landowning castes. The long-term effect of this process is that women get systematically excluded from access to productive resources, which makes for a further decline in their overall status. Jaiswal has convincingly argued that the essential function of the caste system has been to ensure the supply of handicrafts and agricultural labour to upper castes by making upward mobility practically impossible for the menial castes. In the four varna theory, the higher rank enjoyed greater access to non-polluting occupations. If this were the case, it is easy to understand the emergence of the undervaluation of labour as a device to ensure that a ready supply of labour would remain available for the most tedious and physically demanding occupations. In the hierarchy of occupations, those at the lower rungs would remain locked in them simply by virtue of physical labour being devalued. As certain non-menial occupations were valued higher than others, this also served to fortify the ideology of hierarchy as well as legitimize hereditary inequalities. The contempt for Brahmins who peddled their priestly services was an extension of the contempt of upper classes for physical labour (ibid.: 57).

It was in the feudal economy that the status of castes and communities involved in manual work, agriculture and crafts appears to have declined sharply. As a hierarchy of intermediaries developed, who derived their income from the labour on land carried out by primary producers, there was even greater contempt for manual labour and greater exploitation of those engaged in it. Jaiswal writes that this was reflected in the social degradation of peasant communities of the Vaisya varna and their approximation to Shudras in the Smriti literature. Jaiswal argues that those tribes who entered the Brahmanic fold at this stage and subsisted on agricultural labour, came to be regarded as Shudras rather than as Vaishyas in order to emphasize their obligation to serve the higher varnas through manual labour. Also by the beginning of the Christain Era, trade and commerce were being regarded as the distinctive occupations of the Vaishyas, while their association with agriculture and cattle rearing declined by the early medieval period. This shift appears to have been largely responsible for the categorization of peasant communities in the Gupta and post-Gupta periods as Shudras. The roots of this change lay in contempt for manual labour and depression of the peasantry. Indeed the blurring of distinctions between agriculturists of the Vaishya and Shudra categories, led the well-off sections of Vaishyas to turn to trade and commerce, and their giving up of agriculture led to further occupational specialization. It appears that with the emergence of trade as an important factor in the economy, the peasantry became depressed and agriculture was increasingly associated with the

Shudras, the non-Aryan peasant communities being assimilated as Shudras.

While the inclusion of the powerful peasant communities under the Shudra varna had significant consequences, there were important regional variations such as upgrading of the Shudra status in some cases, to distinguish it from the lowly degraded castes. Brahmanical law-givers ranked hierarchically the non-Brahmana castes to rationalize the wide gulf of statuses among them through the *anuloma* and *pratiloma* unions. It is significant that in the *varnasamkara* theory, the impurity of castes does not arise from their adoption of low professions, but the reverse, those of impure birth are condemned to occupations of low status. The theory of purity and pollution arising from birth through approved or disapproved unions, further affirms the basic principles inherent in the varna system by denying access to social prestige and power to impure castes through non-polluting occupations. 'The elaboration of the varna scheme with an accent on birth rather than function was made to provide ideological support to the three tiered stratification of the medieval period' (Jaiswal 1998: 75).

Leacock has pointed out that initially women were profane and uninitiated with regard to men's rituals and men were profane and uninitiated with regard to women's rituals, both sexes enjoying complete autonomy within the imperatives of reciprocity (Leacock 1974: 365). In fact the idea of what is polluting evolved over a long period of time in which material factors such as depression of a community engaged in a particular type of manual labour appears to have played a major role. For instance, leatherwork was not considered low in later Vedic times but contemporary Hindu prejudice against leather as a polluting substance is obviously a later development. This logic could easily be extended to understand the undervaluation of all labour, particularly that done by women.

WOMEN'S LABOUR IN THE CONTEXT OF SANSKRITIZATION

Social Reform and Upward Mobility

A woman must never tire of grinding and pounding
The twelve oxen must keep ploughing the field
Rama's made a great name for himself in the village
While the beast of burden is cutting grass on the mountain.

What fool decided what a woman's life should be?
At her parents' or at her in-laws', she labours for life like an ox.
On seeing the village Bhugaon, the parents married off their daughter.
Now the poor girl's hair's rubbed off with the burden of cow-dung cakes.

Folksongs sung at self-awareness camps of Stri Shakti Mandal, an organization of poor peasant women near Pune, cited in G. Poitevin and H. Rairkar, 1993, *Indian Peasant Women Speak Up*, Bombay: Orient Longman (141; 36)

This section focuses on evidence of Sanskritization processes occurring in the early decades of this century in eastern UP and Bihar among cultivating castes, which found some economic stability under conditions provided by colonial rule. Jaiswal suggests that the concept of Sanskritization is more applicable to colonial times when the link between the caste system and the ruling authority was broken, and the system of production did not need the underpinnings of caste. She points out that in pre-colonial times, the caste system provided cheap labour for agriculture through its repression of menial castes by making available hereditary services of village artisans to peasants, thus reducing overall wage costs. The state was thus able to appropriate more surpluses that also made rulers supportive of the caste system (Jaiswal 1997: 173). On the other hand Srinivas' thesis sees Sanskritization as an accepted avenue of mobility for jatis throughout history, and the emulation by upwardly-mobile caste groups of caste codes and ritual patterns, customs, ideology, and lifestyles of upper castes, particularly when castes acquire the economic wherewithal such as landownership to do so. Clearly Srinivas does not link Sanskritization processes to systems of production (Srinivas 1996: 73-101). As the effort here is to examine the historical evidence for insights into ways in which women are recast when *jatis* redefine and reconstitute themselves, the positions of both these scholars have significant implications for the present study.

In this context Jaiswal and Kulke's (Jaiswal 1997: 173; Kulke 1993: 82-93) counterposing of the Kshatriyaization to the Sanskritization model is pertinent. In the first process, powerful tribal groups or lineages imitated the classical Kshatriya model as well as the process of social change initiated by chiefs and rajas in tribal areas in order to strengthen their economic and political power as well as legitimize their rule. Here the concern is with the specific forms that Sanskritization takes, and particularly the role women are assigned as castes and tribes seek to redefine their identities. The evidence therefore may be seen as illustrative of certain trends, which are likely to have operated in broad contours along similar lines throughout history, wherever conditions have prevailed for the mobility of caste groups.

The 1920s in the United Provinces witnessed a period of intense reformist activity and a flourishing of religious, communal and caste organizations. The Arya Samaj and the Hindu Mahasabha launched their programmes on a large scale by 1923 within which significant gendered notions could be discerned, which were both implicit as well as explicit. While much of these efforts were directed at a reconstruction and redefinition of Hindu masculinity, the deployment of gendered themes and images allows for the emergence of implicit parallel notions of femininity. The Arya Samaj ideology of social reform, the irrelevance of caste distinctions, the message of uplift of low castes and an emphasis on acquired status through education rather than ascriptive social status were spread widely through the leaders of local caste groups. Increasingly, the idea that the sacred thread be viewed as a badge of Hinduhood and not as a status symbol of certain categories of Hindu men or a privilege of certain castes, found its appeal among a large number of lower castes.

In the first two decades of the twentieth century, the *shuddhi* movement for the improvement of the status of lower castes gathered momentum. Within the Arya Samaj ideology, the term '*shuddhi*' for the purification of members of low-castes implied that the low-caste person was given full twice-born status and was accepted as the equal of other Aryas. It also implied the reclamation within the Hindu fold of (a) those low-caste Hindus who had turned to Islam and might be amenable to return to their ancestral faith and (b) those who held a low status within Hinduism which may account for their precarious attachment to the faith (Sharma 1976: 220-1). However, it needs to be emphasized that the Arya Samaj was only one of the various agencies and organizations which influenced the low castes. While the Arya Samaj helped castes such as the Chuhras and Jatavs to acquire some self-respect and identity, the Samaj could often not ensure that this would indeed automatically generate the self-respect of others, or even bring low castes back into the fold of orthodoxy (ibid.: 230).

The 1921 Census Report for the United Provinces noted that, compared to the Christian missionaries, the Arya Samajists were more successful among members of low castes who had recently been able to improve their economic status and who now wanted recognition from the local dominant castes. On the other hand, Christian missionaries had more success among those who had no material prospects (ibid.: 223). This echoes Srinivas' Sanskritization thesis about the significance of a minimum level of economic prosperity that triggers off the aspirations towards improvement in status.

In the new and changed context of colonial rule, many castes emphasized physical and military prowess to replace Eurocentric notions of the emasculated, passive and docile Hindu male population. The *shuddhi* and *sangathan* movements, for instance, evoked legends and myths of Rajput valour and a distant past in which the Hindu male epitomized ideal perfection, and a past that evoked militant Kshatriya virtues was appropriated for a new narrative. As a result, a large number of gymnasiums and *akharas* for wrestling and swordfighting were set up in various localities of cities such as Varanasi and Allahabad, and these physical culture clubs came to symbolize the prowess of the Hindu male and popularized the Kshatriya dharma.

Here I draw on the thesis that in the late nineteenth and early twentieth centuries, Sanskritization occurred in the context of a growing emphasis on Vaishnava beliefs and practices, within Hinduism. Rama and Krishna, avatars of Vishnu, were representatives of a distinct martial Kshatriya tradition where the lineages of the sun and moon (Suryavanshis and Chandravanshis) were the key in the formation of new caste identities as warrior nobles (Pinch 1996: 12).

Vaishnavism created the religio-philosophical space wherein colonialism could be critiqued. Contrary to western allegations that Hindusim was otherworldly and advocated salvation through renunciation, Vaishnavism urged householders to confront problems, and prepared them to fight. It may not be out of place to recall that the British had an active hand in promoting an image of Hinduism, as aloof to worldly affairs. Warren Hastings, in the wake of Fakir and Sannyasi rebellions (1760s and 1770s) marshalled an image of the ideal sadhu as essentially calm, immersed in his search for right knowledge, and generally keeping himself above temporal concerns. Devotion to Rama and Krishna allowed for the appropriation of suitable Kshatriya symbols and origin myths necessary for Sanskritization, providing a legitimizing context within which jati reformers could direct change, accompanied with strictures placed on women which evoked martial traditions and were quite at variance with the prevailing cosmogonies of cultivating castes. In the long run, these processes had serious implications for women's productive roles as well as access to resources.

In a later chapter I shall see how middle-caste peasants, the Yadavas, Koeris, and Kurmis, were known to be efficient cultivators and owed their prosperity and competence to family labour, including that of women. Such tenants were much in demand by landlords. Koeris, for instance, were known for cash crop agriculture and propounded the myth that they were created by Shiva to tend the vegetable gardens of Benaras (Risley 1892: 501). On the varna scale, such cultivating castes represented the fourth category, the Shudras, debarred from wearing the sacred thread (because of the devaluation of all physical labour in the caste scheme). Broadly, the agrarian hierarchy corresponded with the caste hierarchy so that the Brahmins and Kshatriyas held the proprietary rights in land while the bulk of tenants, both occupancy and tenants-at-will, were Shudra jatis such as Yadavas, Koeris, Kurmis, and Kahars. In eastern UP and Bihar, Shudras comprised approximately 60 per cent of the Hindu population.

Vaishnava ideas and culture undermined the hierarchy implicit in caste and provided the space within which reformers could question certain institutions (Pinch 1996: 76). In the *akharas* of the Ramnandi *sampradaya*, sacred thread ceremonies for the Shudras could take place—all this provided the backdrop for social change (ibid.). Hence different jatis emphasized different elements of the Vaishnava culture such as eschewing of meat and alcohol or the emphasis on legendry Kshatriya valour and its reassertion in the colonial context. The Koeris for instance, rejected their Shiva-oriented origin myth and by the 1920s were espousing a Kushwaha Kshatriya identity based on kin ties with Rama through one of his sons, Kush. This identity was stretched out to include Kacchwaha, Kachhi and Murao agriculturists, other significant agriculturist castes of UP (Pinch 1996: 91-2). Their jati pamphlet portrayed the Koeri woman as steadfast, loyal and devoted in the true traditions of Kshatriya women, who showed courage in battle and immolated themselves rather than succumb to the enemy (ibid.).

Another prominent agricultural caste in the region, the Yadavas, claimed descent from Raja Yadu, thereby asserting kinship with Krishna and encompassing the Ahir, Gop, Gopal, and Sadgop jatis. In south Bihar for instance, the Yadavas, also known as Goalas, were required to offer *begar* (unpaid customary labour) to the Bhumihar Brahmin landlords. 'As cowherds, milk-sellers, labourers, palanquin bearers, and tenants, they were economically dependent on and politically subservient to the locally dominant landowning castes' (Rao 1979: 132). The Yadava caste sought to overcome its ritual disabilities not only by claiming Kshatriya status and descent from the Yadu dynasty, but by adopting Arya Samaj practices as well. A notable feature of the spread of Arya Samaj practices was the *janeo* movement wherein the wearing of the sacred thread was adopted in public. As this meant organized activity, it attracted the attention of the higher castes and around 1912, there were violent riots in which, Bhumihar Brahmins invaded the public functions of the Ahirs with *lathis* and rifles and imposed collective fines, and filed civil and criminal suits against the Ahirs (ibid.: 134).

The Yadava movement had a vast interregional spread which attempted to submerge the regional names in favour of an all-India Yadava identity. Within this broadly defined Yadava identity, at least in the United Provinces and Bihar, the well-off sections of the caste insisted that women be prohibited from selling cow-dung cakes or milk in the weekly markets and bazaars, and that in all respects they should emulate the practices of the women of upper castes. Rao, in his discussion of the Yadava movement, does not make clear whether or not restrictions began to be placed on widow remarriage and divorce as these had previously been permitted among the Yadavas. He does suggest that child marriages and dowries began to pose problems especially when Western-educated Yadava leaders started condemning them. The all-India Yadava Mahasabha pointed out the evils of child marriage and stressed the virtue of unostentatious ceremonies and condemned the funerary feasts, which were seen as expensive and representative of Brahmin exploitation (ibid.: 141). As class differentiation within the caste appears to have been considerable, Yadava Kshatriya identity could succeed only to the extent that economic considerations allowed. In the ritual sphere, the caste was able to obtain the services of Brahmins and Nais to perform the requisite *dwija* ceremonies, though efforts to prevent women's most visible participation in cattle rearing, agriculture and marketing of produce could not be uniformly enforced—economic dependence on the labour of women was considerable among these castes. To do away with this labour would have meant a decline in economic conditions, which only the most prosperous sections of Yadavas could afford. Nevertheless, the emulation of upper-caste seclusion for women remained an important aspiration for these jatis. On the other hand, the underlying rationale for caste hierarchy, namely the undervaluation of physical labour, particularly ploughing, began to be seriously questioned as Yadavas appeared in the fields wearing the sacred thread.

Reform movements during this period had in common serious attempts to redefine physical labour (Pinch 1996: 75). Jati reformers appear to have uniformly asserted that agricultural work was in no way undignified. In 1907 a Kurmi pamphlet, for instance, stated that as agriculture is associated with the Earth, it is a noble vocation (Pawar: 1933). In 1927, another pamphlet argued that since Maharaja Janak, the father of Sita, practised agriculture, farming could not be an obstacle to Kshatriyahood. Similarly, non-agricultural Shudra jatis were urged to take pride in their technical and artisanal skills. The Kahar reformers argued that as water had to be drawn and carried by all castes everyday, it could by no means be considered degrading. The emphasis on the dignity of physical work and the significance of labour enabled many castes to take advantage of the economic opportunities of the colonial period. Many used Brahmanical texts and interpretations to make their case. This represents only one of the ways in which Sanskritization was furthered. This emphasis also called into question age-old notions about the degrading nature of physical labour, particularly the act of preparing the field and wielding the plough (Pinch 1996: 107-12). It questioned the very basis of the hierarchy, in which the twice-born castes are superior by virtue of their distance from physical labour, especially ploughing, a hierarchy reinforced by the political control that the superior castes wielded over the products of the land and the products of others' labour. This line of questioning became possible within a social milieu where opposition to landed authority had become something like the norm. In times of crisis or heightened political consciousness, ritualistic barriers could be broken, as in the case of Bhumihar Brahmin women who took up ploughing in Bihar in the 1930s (Kumar 2001).

The struggle for secured tenancy in Majhiyawan (Gaya), Bihar, in 1939-40, became witness to a withering away of the century-old prohibition on ploughing for women (of all castes along with men of upper castes). Just before the onset of the paddy season the fields were captured by the zamindar and he would not allow tenants to cultivate them. A Restraint Order from the court prohibited tenants from ploughing. Breaking the court order would have meant inviting violence either from the zamindar or the court/state, or both but women from tenant families captured the land and ploughed it. Soon lower-caste women joined them. Similar reports were heard from Ghosrawan, Patna (ibid.: 250-1).

It has been argued that the broader agendas of the jati reformers were education, cultural and religious reform, economic frugality, social and physical cleanliness and, above all, self-respect. Folksongs of the period reflect that in accordance with the changing times, labouring castes were becoming increasingly aware of their collective strength. Having realized this strength, upper castes who did not participate in production were threatened, as is evident in the following Bhojpuri folksong which is still remembered and sung by the generation of freedom-fighters in western Bihar (ibid.).

Aisan awata samaiya harawa jote ke pari
Bin har jote phasal na hoihen
Na hi upaji dhan
Babulog sab harawa jotihen
Babuni ropihen dhan
Harawa jote ke pari.

The time is approaching when everyone will have to plough.
Unless the land is ploughed, neither crops
nor paddy will grow.
Upper-caste men will plough the land themselves
Upper-caste women will replant paddy seedlings.
Ploughing will have to be done by all.

It is in the sphere of women's social and economic behaviour that jati reformers of the period appear to have focused attention, with a view to elevating the status of the entire caste. Reformers spelt out a range of restrictions for women: Yadavas were urged to halt the rule of women in the home; restrictions were placed on women singing in public or viewing a *barat,* attending festivals and fairs where the risk of being dishonoured in large crowds prevailed, or even buying bangles from male bangle sellers. In addition, as noted above, Yadava women were to be debarred from peddling milk and cow-dung cakes in the bazaars. Kurmis were cautioned against educating women, as this would have a negative effect on children, household work, and on the growth of loving relationships between husbands and wives (Pinch 1996: 125).

The Case of the Kurmi Caste

Here I present the Kurmi caste association's concerns as a case which affords insights into the perceptions of a dominant peasant caste, its efforts to deal with some of these practices, and search for status within the hierarchy of castes. The Kurmi Sangh's position on various issues reveals the centrality of the woman in the efforts of a caste to reformulate its identity. The Kurmi case provides an interesting example of the manner in which women's productive activity was sought to be controlled in the caste's collective efforts at mobility. While control over women's sexuality has always been recognized as a means of maintaining caste position within the hierarchy, less acknowledged is that often these controls restrict women's productivity and seem to systematically alienate women from knowledge and skills. Restrictions placed on Kurmi women by the Sangh, which was an acceptance of the value system and ideology of upper castes (where productive labour is devalued), resulted in a loss of skills requiring that males be in a position to do without women's productive contributions. While more prosperous castes such as Yadavas, Koeris and Kurmis could afford this, many others were simply unable to withdraw women from work.

The Kurmi Sangh was formed at the initiative of Baba Ramchandra. Documentary evidence on the Sangh is of great sociological value as it provides insights into the manner in which caste solidarity was achieved for both social and political gains, and reveals this peasant leader's vision.[3] Baba Ramchandra stressed the Kurmi Sangh's collective functions in uniting together people of common occupational and economic interests. Once cohesion within the different castes such as Kurmis, Koeris, Pasis, Chamars, etc., could be achieved, it was believed that these groups would become stronger. In the Baba's vision, different caste groups united under the leadership of their *panchayats*, could effectively resist the injustices of the system. The membership fee of the *panchayat* was 1 *seer* grain and 1 oz. cotton wool (*Baba Ramchandra Papers, 1933-50*, NMML).

In Awadh the insecurity of tenure which came to characterize conditions under colonial rule meant considerable loss in status for a caste which had been known for its industry and skill as well as small proprietary holdings as minor zamindars. In contrast to other Sanskritizing caste groups during the same period mentioned above, many Kurmi cultivators of Awadh were actually facing a decline in economic prosperity owing to precarious tenurial legislations which rendered 90 per cent of Awadh tenants into tenants-at-will. On the other hand as it was the Awadhiya Kurmis who could boast of zamindari rights in Awadh and thus a status marginally at par with *dwija* proprietary castes of the region, the reasons to reinstate, fortify and elevate their position in the social hierarchy appear to have been particularly imminent in their case.

To ensure that high-caste men would not exploit women of the cultivating castes, Baba Ramchandra laid down that (a) women should work on their own lands and fields and not for others, unless they were paid full wages; (b) women should be prevented from attending bazaars as there was danger of losing chastity in such gatherings; (c) couples should be legally separated if they did not get along in marriage; and (d) to improve the lot of women, men must be reformed (ibid.).

The first two injunctions were direct attempts to control women's access to public spaces, and reflect the caste's concern with women's chastity, thereby elevating the caste's position. Efforts to resist extra-economic coercion (by which *begari* fell largely to the lot of peasant women) were possible only through restrictions on women working for others. Restrictions on women's access to other public spaces such as bazaars were in emulation of upper-caste norms. The sanctity of the marriage tie was sought to be enforced by curbs on the old leeway and flexibility in the face of intolerable unions. Thus many of the supposed reforms targeted women and encouraged the adoption of an ideology that placed severe restrictions on them.

The Case of the Kalwars

The Kalwars were a caste of liquor-brewers and dealers who decided to give up the manufacture, sale and consumption of alcohol altogether, in an effort to improve their status. The caste attempted to evolve a new identity by adopting a new surname, Jaiswal. At a well-attended meeting of the jati advertised as the Kalwar Kshatriya Mahasabha in Allahabad held on 7, 8 and 9 February 1921, the jati members were told 'You are the descendants of Kulin Aryas, does this not inspire you to great things?' They were urged to give up their 'bad customs' and take to education. In a reference to Gandhi's position on alcohol, caste members were urged to shun it: drinking and offering alcohol to others is the greatest sin. The appeal to those members assumed to be reluctant to leave the caste trade was, 'do not become money hungry monsters.' Appeals were made to subscribe to 'good dharma, which stays with one forever'. On the second day of the Mahasabha, which coincided with the public auction of liquor in Allahabad city, the tone was congratulatory towards those who did not take the contract for supplying liquor to the city and thus gave up the opportunity to earn huge sums of money. Appeals were made to the caste to shun those brethren who had obtained contracts for selling liquor or were employed by contractors. Further, in a concerted drive for the education of youngsters, it was decided that each household of the thousand-household strong community donate 4 *annas* per month. In case this was not feasible, women were asked to set aside, each time rice was to be prepared, one fistful of rice for the education of boys of the caste. Further, a bank was to be opened and 10 per cent of the profit set aside yearly for the education of boys. The concern for education predictably remained confined to male members of the community. It is often from the unstated and the unexpressed that many inferences can be drawn about gender discrimination.

Reform was the rallying cry of many middle and lower castes. Caste leaders reflected on the best strategies to improve their status, and attempts to drop association with terms such as Vaishya and Kalwar were considered. A reference was made to a delegation sent to one Mahajan Hitkarni Sabha, which ruled that the ancestors of the caste had prepared liquor with the use of *kal* (pressing machines) which is how the caste got its name. Owing to its derogatory connotations, it was suggested that the caste drop the name Kalwar in favour of Jaiswal. Further,

Our sanatan dharma says that we are Kshatriyas, then why should we call ourselves Vaishyas? Our ancestors were Brahmins who left their community/kin to face this downfall. From that day we have become bereft of good upbringing and have left the practice of reading Vedas. . . . Now we have acquired knowledge about our lost Kshatriyaness, then why not proclaim ourselves Kshatriyas as we really are?

It was proposed to adopt the title of Somvanshiya Kshatriya. Caste members were urged to purge their names of suffixes such as Lala, used by Vaishyas, and adopt prefixes such as Kunwar and Thakur instead. Surnames such as Dhwaja, Thakur and Singh were recommended.

Apart from a discussion on the origins of the Jaiswal, their geographical spread and attempt to seek fictive kinship ties with other prosperous Jaiswal communities in the Deccan, Rewa State, etc., there was an attempt to make a distinction between those members of the caste who had given up the liquor trade and called themselves Chowdhri, elevated their status and broke off all commensal and affinal links from those who continued with the liquor trade. Finally, these caste members were Shiva and Shakti followers, but had in recent years, under the considerable influence of Vaishnavism and the Arya Samaj, adopted changes in their practices.

'An open letter to the Brahmins of Rajapuri', written by Ganga Prasad Jayaswal in 1928, is of considerable interest. It is in response to the Brahmins' violent objections to the Kalwars' claims to *janeo* (sacred thread) (Jayaswal 1928). The Kalwars of Dumraon asserted their right to wear the sacred thread on the grounds that it is prescribed for all *dwijas*. Interestingly, in support of their right to do so, the Kalwars cited and invoked several classical Brahmanical texts, which actually reinforce and legitimize Brahman ritual superiority. The letter writer quotes from the *Ramcharitmanas, Skanda Purana*, *Padma Purana*, and *Narada Samhita*, recalling the words of Vasistha, Angira or Vyas which underline the significance of the sacred thread for the twice-born. In the absence of *janeo,* ritual impurity is likely to annul even the most pious deeds such as pilgrimage and *daan* of any sort including *annadaan*. For instance, the *Narada Samhita's* assertion that the onus to purify the *yajman* through the ritual of *yagnopavita* lies on the *purohit*, is cited in support of the Kalwar claims. Inability to do so implies that the *purohit* would accompany the *yajman* to hell. While the texts cited seem to be reaffirming Brahman ritual superiority, the letter in question could be read as an inversion—in asserting Kalwar claims to also don the sacred thread, Brahmin superiority is called into question and the edifice of caste hierarchy is dismantled.

Ganga Prasad's letter offers unique insights into another less known dimension of the strivings for upward mobility, namely the reactions and responses of other castes. The letter mentions the atrocities perpetrated by the local Brahmin community on Kalwars who dared to don the sacred thread. It appears that the *janeos* were forcibly snatched off and broken, the people were denied water from the village wells and the Nai, Dhobi, Kahar and Bhangi were also forced to deny services to them. At the Shri Nav Yuvak Haihay-Kshatriya Hitkarini Sabha which met on 26 and 27 May 1928, the ceremony of mass *yagnopavita* was disrupted by stone pelting, the hurling of abuses and the humiliation of guests who included the Kalwar preachers and singers of bhajans. Volunteers were roughed up and people were prevented from using the fields for defecation. Clearly the attempt at Sanskritization did not go unchallenged and the resistance by upper castes was marked by physical atrocities meted out to upwardly-mobile castes.

Sharma makes a distinction between the Hinduizing efforts of the Arya Samaj as opposed to Sankritization efforts. To rural Hindus whom the Arya Samaj sought to uplift, the sacred thread actually held a different meaning than it did for Arya Samajis, for whom it was a symbol of initiation as a Hindu to the Arya Samaj. For rural Hindus it was a sign of membership to a clean caste and meant that low castes were asserting their right to a higher status than formerly accorded. In many such cases this led to low-caste Arya Samaj converts being beaten up, largely because the urban missionaries of the Samaj were in no position to offer protection to those converted (Sharma 1976: 235).

The emerging vernacular press in the province reproduced and strengthened a construction of the woman which was increasingly detached from productive resources and activities. Scores of journals, primers, and guidebooks appeared, to spread a masculinist construction of the ideal woman who had no independence, no economic leverage, and was totally subservient to the male world. It is not surprising that mainly upper-caste males wrote primers emphasizing the housekeeping skills of the good woman as in

Kanyamanoranjan, or *Naarisudasha Pravartak* (Bankelal 1909). The latter has detailed instructions through rhymes, anecdotes and letters for women of varied backgrounds, ranging from *thagini*, the cheat, *chatori*, the greedy one, to widows, menstruating, pregnant, post-natal/lactating women, mothers of sons, and aged women.

In upcoming urban areas upper castes were seen to uphold the sanctity of marriage as evidenced in the chaste, modest, and secluded demeanour of upper-caste women. In contrast, the poor were supposed to live in temporary marriages, experiencing frequent divorces and desertions (Sen 1999: 8-9). Further, the ideology of domesticity stripped the notion of femininity of its labour content and denuded its economic value for the household. 'The physical and social invisibility of elite women's work underwrote the denigration of women's remunerated work' (ibid.: 9). This is why, despite increased visibility of poor women's work in high migration areas, they could not benefit much. Their labour and income continued to be viewed as 'supplementary' to the 'main bread winner' who was quintessentially male. As a mark of status, however, the ideology of domesticity did not prevent poor women from working but promoted the claims of middle-class women to the prized domain of exclusive housewifery and childcare (ibid.).[4]

Hence two stereotypes of women were being constructed. In the first case, women who could afford not to work were being defined through the primers as 'ideal women' while 'working women' who were remunerated for their services were denigrated owing to the pervasive devaluation of all manual labour.

CONCLUSION

Modern industry has replaced petty production, which favoured craft-exclusiveness on a non-competitive basis. It has eroded notions of caste hierarchy and untouchability and the taboos on interdining. But the prohibition of inter-caste marriage is still observed widely, for it is not in conflict with the capitalist mode of production. On the contrary, caste endogamy actually is marriage on considerations of wealth, power, status and as such is well impregnated with the capitalist value system (Jaiswal 1998: 20).

Similarly the patron-client nexus of the *jajmani* type is being replaced by the impersonal monetary forms of exchange, under the influence of market forces. On the other hand, caste ideology is gaining strength for economic and political reasons (ibid.). In Miriam Sharma's analysis of caste, class and gender in a UP village, caste and class were found to overlap and remain congruent. Land and power was concentrated in the hands of Bhumihars while Chamars remained deprived of these. Sharma shows how rich and poor women experience gender oppression in different ways and are placed in subordinate positions at different levels in the interaction of class and gender. Sharma's evidence shows that women are increasingly losing control over productive resources and over the labour process and production. This has eroded the material base of women's subsistence and adversely affected their status. Sharma's findings are that (a) the increased economic independence and security of men secures only increased dependence and restriction in the lives of women; (b) with loss of their role and any chance for capital accumulation, women's status gets devalued; (c) this is most apparent in the enhanced domestic status of Chamar women and the enhanced public status of the Bhumihars (Sharma 1985: 57-88).

Chowdhry's analysis of the current phase of stringent enforcement of caste and kinship codes in rural Haryana through closer surveillance of marriage alliances, suggests the strengthening of caste, and its continuing leverage in wider society and polity. As any breach in caste linkages is seen as bringing down the status of not only the immediate family but also the clan and the entire caste group, caste and sexual codes are being strictly enforced in today's context with dangerous violent consequences particularly for women who challenge them (Chowdhry 1997: 1019). As it has already been seen, woman's sexuality has always been central to codes of caste purity, status and hierarchy. While claims to tradition, culture and honour are commonly invoked by castes across the hierarchy, they are especially articulated by those groups who stand to benefit most by bolstering them. Chowdhry links this tendency to the insecurities created by the enablement of daughters to inherit landed property (ibid.). As the class and gender component within the caste system has created inter-caste and intra-caste differentiation, inequalities and status distinctions, these aspects need further probing. Clearly the interface between caste, class and gender is crucial in the understanding of caste system as it exists today.

This chapter has examined historical processes by which access to land has been denied to women. This denial is crucial in understanding questions and issues pertaining to the emergence of patriarchal class divisions and the state. The departure from communal modes of ownership to individual ownership marked women's systematic exclusion from land and productive resources. As society became more complex and hierarchical, the consolidation of endogamous caste practices and women's exclusion from land was further cemented. Even in the modern period, when caste identities were being reaffirmed and redefined, and miniscule efforts to challenge the devaluation of physical labour came about, women's exclusion from resources continued. All this had a negative impact on women since the purity of a caste was defined in terms of women's purity. Instead of emphasizing women's capacity to produce, the effort was to tie them down to their reproductive and home-making roles, as a result of aspirations to upward mobility. This became possible only because women's labour had become invisible.

As peasant differentiation intensifies, women are further excluded from productive resources. The process of marginalization was complete within caste ideologies, which, in seeking to redefine social identities, devalued women's labour. A study of peasant differentiation would be incomplete without placing women at the centre of the enquiry—which is the theme explored in the next chapter.

NOTES

1. N. Banerjee, 'The Structural Adjustment Programme and Women's Economic Empowerment', in N. Rao, L. Rurup and R. Sudarshan (eds.), *Sites of Change: The Structural Context for Empowering Women in India*. FES and UNDP, New Delhi, 1996.
2. Basham suggests the influence of *ratnins* in the growth of the state in the later Vedic times. *Ratnins* or jewel-bearers from among the relatives, courtiers and palace officials of the king were looked upon as so significant, that at the king's coronation, special sacrifices were performed to ensure their loyalty. The list of *ratnins* included the *purohit* or chief priest of the palace, the general, the chamberlain, the king's charioteer and various influential palace servants (Basham 1967: 43).
3. Similarly Bihar in the 1930s witnessed the emergence of a parallel organization, the Triveni Sangh, consisting of Yadavas, Kurmis and Koeris.

The Triveni Sangh was largely a response of the kisans to the Bihar Kisan Sabha led by Sahajanand Saraswati, which was perceived as being dominated by upper caste Bhumihars (Kumar 2001).

4. In the wake of the industrial revolution, the metropolis witnessed a substantial change in its society. The valorization of domesticity occurred with denigration of women's labour within and outside the boundaries of the home. See, among others, Joan W. Scott and Louise A. Tilly, 'Women's Work and Family in Nineteenth Century Europe', *Comparative Studies in Society and History* 17 (1975); Judith K. Brown, 'A Note on the Division of Labor by Sex', *American Anthropologist* 72 (1970).

CHAPTER 2

Peasant Differentiation in Awadh: Making Women Visible

Outdoor work puts a strain on your feet.
Work in the house breaks your back.

I went to work; but what is the value of my work?
Brother, I'm telling you, I'm as good as any man.
(*folksong*)

Who bothers to shed tears
Over the woman who dies everyday? (*saying*)

Songs and sayings shared by members of Stri Shakti Mandal, an organization of poor peasant women near Pune, cited in G. Poitevin and H. Rairkar, 1993, *Indian Peasant Women Speak Up*, Bombay: Orient Longman (141-4)

Within the rich historical literature on colonial India, the nature of regional agrarian relations has been well documented, yet women's roles in agrarian production remain obscure (Bhattacharya 1985; Breman 1979; Guha 1981; Ludden 1985). Assumptions of gender neutrality in accounts of the restructuring of rural society as a consequence of colonial rule have rendered invisible the women in these processes. As a consequence, many of the discussions portray (a) the peasant as predominantly male and (b) the peasantry as undifferentiated and largely homogenous. The generic term 'peasantry' tends to obscure class differentiation and distinctions, blurring the variety and range within it. On the other hand when caste is seen as a form of relations of production, the exploitative relations that emerge from the satisfaction of subsistence needs and appropriation of surpluses, are highlighted. It is the contention here that if access to and control over productive resources as well as productive activity and skills of women are factored into the analysis, the differentiation within the class of peasantry (as a whole), appears in sharper relief.

The tendency to view the peasantry as undifferentiated which pervades historical records, a legacy of the colonial state, has found resonance even in current scholarship. The access to and control over productive resources exercised by different classes and castes of women in the agrarian structure has therefore to be teased out of the existing data. Such an exercise has fruitful and far-reaching implications not only for historical research but also in the analysis of processes of change in contemporary society. In recent years, for instance, the political implications of viewing the peasantry as undifferentiated and homogenous were in evidence in the New Farmers Movements of the 1980s, where the interests of rich peasants were projected as representative of the entire body of peasantry, at the cost of the interests of marginal and small farmers and agricultural labourers. The peasantry was recast as a non-economic cultural category bereft of its historical character (Brass 1993: 15).

This chapter argues that the access of women to productive resources and the nature of their involvement in production, are necessary to understand the totality of agrarian relations historically. Critiquing the conventional classification of households by landholding size as an insufficient measure of differentiation, Utsa Patnaik has developed the labour exploitation index as a more meaningful alternative, wherein classes within the cultivating peasantry are identified by inquiring into the degree of working for others or of employing others' labour relative to self-employment (Patnaik 1987, 1991). Pushing this line of enquiry further, I investigate the centrality of the utilization of women's productivity in the increasing differentiation between classes.

My focus is on the nature of agrarian relations existing in the Awadh region, with particular emphasis on the Faizabad district on the eve of colonial rule. This will place in perspective the changes which arose as a consequence of British intervention in 1856. Through an examination of peasant women's roles in agrarian production, some explanations for their invisibility are offered. In exploring the interlinkages between caste, class and gender, my effort is to locate peasant women within the institutions and practices of their daily lives. While peasant women's contributions and roles appear only tangentially in the debates which preceded the colonial legislation, they provide a significant backdrop to understanding the logic which informed peasant society. Thus, for instance, how was colonial concern with raising rents to the maximum reconciled with the traditional privileges enjoyed by certain categories of resident and high-caste peasants? My enquiry explores the extent to which the logic of these privileges was a function of women's roles within the peasant economy structured by caste.

The historical evidence is therefore deployed not to reconstruct the historical specificity of a given social formation but to point to certain processes and trends, which may be valid across historical periods and epochs. The questions raised by the historical evidence are posed as tentative hypotheses requiring further research, investigations and testing in the field.

PEASANT DIFFERENTIATION: THE RESIDENCE FACTOR

Administrative inquiries undertaken soon after the annexation of Awadh in 1856 revealed the nature of rights traditionally enjoyed by different cultivators. It was on this base that colonial rule erected a new and modified edifice. From these accounts it is possible to reconstruct the differentiating features among the peasantry, as well as (to an extent) the nature of women's roles in agrarian production.

It was found that cultivators in the province had been cultivating the fields for years and sometimes even for generations. As land was abundant and labour scarce, cultivators could not leave the land nor refuse to cultivate it. Moreover different strata in the agrarian structure had different rights over the land and its produce, and there was no exclusive right of property. Traditionally, landlords had recognized the rights of cultivators to hold their lands in perpetuity, and such rights were hereditary. However peasants could rarely sell, abandon or dispose of their lands (Habib 1963). The agrarian structure was characterized by a layering of rights in land, different sets of rights being enjoyed by different groups, rather than individual proprietorship to the exclusion of all others. There appeared to be many safeguards against peasants being evicted from holdings, which they had been cultivating for long. Irfan Habib

(1963) has shown how, with land abundant and labour scarce, industrious peasants were much sought after and, in practice at least, it was rather rare for landlords to actually evict a peasant. In fact such a move by the landlord would have militated against the peasants' own legitimate 'interest' in the soil. As it will be seen, colonial rule on the other hand, legitimized arbitrary evictions and created conditions in which peasant women's insecurities were further enhanced.

In the historical evidence relating to the eve of British rule, a fundamental distinction is recognized between the *khudkast* (resident) or permanent peasants who cultivated their own village lands and the *pahikasht* peasants who came from neighbouring villages. The fact of residence within the village was crucial as it determined a range of other attributes associated with membership in a village community, as well as privileges and rights of cultivators. In Faizabad, the majority of *khudkasht* and *pahikasht* peasants were (in order of numerical strength) Ahirs, Brahmins, Rajputs, Kurmis, Kahars, Muraos, Kewats and Koeris (Crooke 1975). According to the 1901 census, the Hindu population of Faizabad included 96 castes, of which 23 had a strength exceeding 1,00,000 persons each. The top and bottom rungs of the hierarchy were occupied by Brahmins and Chamars respectively, and these two castes had the greatest numerical strength in Faizabad. The Chamars, leather workers, were largely engaged as agricultural labourers on the lands of high-caste peasants and landlords. A close numerical second were the Brahmins of the Saryupari sub-caste who were engaged in agriculture though ritual sanctions forced them to hire labour for cultivation. From long they had enjoyed 25 per cent reduction in rent rates. This covered the extra expenditure they were forced to incur in hiring labour.

An analysis of the features of *khudkasht* peasants reflects the immense value of such cultivators and the privileges enjoyed by them may be seen as the unstated acknowledgement of their value for landlords. The fact that *khudkasht* cultivators resided in the village with their *chapperband* (homesteads) located on its territory, implied a degree of permanency and rootedness within the village, and thus their vested interest in ensuring maximum productivity. This self-interest of *khudkasht* peasants made them eminently desirable in the eyes of landlords who were consequently assured of continued cultivation with inputs such as ploughs, oxen and seed provided by the cultivators themselves. That *khudkasht* cultivators possessed their own factors of production, including cattle and bullocks, further ensured that fields would also be well-manured.

To maximize productivity from the land, and in peak seasons of agricultural activity when extra hands were a necessity, *khudkasht* cultivators could always enlist the labour of family members, women and children of the household. Where the cultivators also belonged to traditional cultivating castes, it was understood that their women's labour in the fields would be readily available. Unlike high-caste peasant women's taboos with respect to working in the fields, *khudkasht* households managed to save on wages of agricultural labour. This underscored the advantages of the *khudkasht* peasant for the landlord.

A brief review of agricultural operations in the Awadh countryside dependent on women's labour puts into perspective the varied and complex contributions of women in agriculture, most of which have existed without much change through colonial times into the present day. Except for the act of ploughing, women's participation was evident in varied measure in the tasks of tilling, sowing, manuring, irrigating fields, weeding, cutting and reaping, carrying and transporting, threshing, winnowing and storing (Jafri 1931: 244). It was common for the woman of the peasant household to walk behind the man wielding the plough in order to scatter the seeds in the furrows so created. Weeding was carried out by girls, young boys and women family members using a *khurpi* or small hand hoe (ibid.: 260). Female labour was particularly called upon for this function, owing to the fact that women were regarded as having the patience required for this task. Women used to till the land with a *kudar* or sharp pointed axe to loosen the earth around the roots of plants. Where irrigation was done from ponds, *jhils*, tanks and wells, *kiaries* or water channels were made to distribute water at regular intervals. Women prepared the *kiaries* or beds with raised borders to retain the water. Their labour was enlisted to see that water was evenly distributed in the fields, by scraping the water channels periodically with *phaories* or spades. Where irrigation was done by lifts, water was made to collect in a sort of reservoir. The entire operation required five individuals to work the lift, two to work at raising the baskets, two as relief and one to distribute the water (ibid.: 260-5). The latter was invariably a woman.

At harvest time, women cut the crop using the *hasiya* or sickle. The reaped crop was carried to the threshing floor by men and women and was either trodden out by oxen, or beaten by the women with sticks. In the case of small grain, women separated the chaff with their feet by treading over small quantities. Winnowing was entirely done by women. The beaten grain was lifted and let to fall in a current of wind. The grain being heavy fell to the ground, while the lighter fragments of chaff were blown away into another heap. Just before storing, the grain was once again tossed in a *soup* or sieve by the womenfolk to clear it of impurities. If the grain had to be ground before storing, or other processing was required, these tasks essentially fell upon the women according to household requirements.

It was largely the women of cultivating castes such as Kacchis, Koeris and Kurmis who contributed to all the agricultural operations mentioned above, with the exception of ploughing. Their unique partnership with men in all the agricultural operations, led Jafri to reflect that 'it is this coordination which has made these classes unique in cultivation' (ibid.: 210). He further points out that the young of such families were early socialized in their productive roles. Starting from a very young age, cultivators' sons took breakfast to their fathers in the field, taking over this task from mothers; prepared tobacco for the *hukka*; grazed cattle in the afternoon and cared for them, then drove them back after the day's work. Slightly older boys helped fathers in the field, especially at weeding and usually at the age of fourteen, took their place as men in the agricultural cycle. Girls on the other hand were socialized into cleaning floors and pots, carrying water and looking after infants (ibid.: 210).

In Faizabad, Kurmis were most valued by landlords. Owing to their skill in agriculture, this was a caste which was rarely evicted. The fact that they paid a rent higher than both Brahmins and Rajputs made them even more attractive. Kurmis had a reputation for building fine wells and several Awadh district Gazetteers described them as hardworking, intelligent and as cultivators of the highest order (Nevill 1905). In Faizabad, Kurmis also had the reputation of being a dangerous body when roused, of keeping to themselves and of combining better than other castes (ibid.). The productivity of a Kurmi household appears to have been high, as Kurmi women had no restrictions on labouring in the fields. Awadh folklore provides instances of Kurmi women's agricultural abilities thus:

Bhali jat Kurmi, Khurpi Nath Khet Niarawe apan pi ke saath

> The kurmi woman is an asset—with her implements she accompanies her husband for weeding the fields. (Crooke 1975, vol. III: 354)

The Kurmi woman's interest in the welfare of the crop was expressed in the following manner:

ek pan jo barse swati
Kurmi pahire sore ke pati

> With the first shower in Swati, the Kurmi woman wears rings of gold. (ibid.)

Even today, the discerning eye can identify differences between fields cultivated by different castes: the well-tended neat rows of the Koeris and Kurmi fields reflect women's work. Among Koeri and Kurmis, entire households engage in vegetable cultivation and the women's contribution is crucial. There are instances of fields being harvested in the morning, ploughed by midday and sown with the new crop before sunset, particularly where cabbages and cauliflower are cultivated for export. On the other hand, diseased plants, untended and weed-ridden beds and uneven irrigation channels are attributed in public consciousness to the upper castes for whom women's labour has traditionally been unavailable.

A reference from the year 1928 pertains to the productive activity in the household of a *khudkast* peasant, Ram Din of the Ahir cultivating caste from village Argaja Pandeypur, in neighbouring Mirzapur. The family consisted of five men, five women, and six children and they cultivated 20.5 *bighas* of land in 1928. The family owned two ploughs and in *kharif*, the family ploughed the field ten times and levelled it six times. Nine people were permanently engaged in *kharif.* Among family members, five men and four women were involved in production round the year. In addition, for reaping (which was conducted over four days) four women agricultural labourers were hired. While watering was not required in this season, weeding was done three times, entirely with the help of family labour. Similarly for threshing which was done over ten days, no extra hands were required.

For the *rabi* crop, the field was ploughed eight times and levelled six times. Five men and four women of the house were engaged in the operations, and four women were hired to reap for four days. The field was irrigated ten times but no extra hand was engaged. Rabi crops do not require weeding (Jafri 1931: 419). It is clear from the above evidence that cooperation between men and women of peasant castes was crucial for cultivation and enabled *khudkasht* households to save on hired labour. The above evidence also suggests that the industry and labour of women and its ready availability in the case of middle-peasant castes would have contributed in no small measure to the attractiveness of these communities for landlords. The worth of such cultivators for landlords may be assessed from the advantages and privileges traditionally enjoyed by *khudkasht* peasants.

Advantages Enjoyed by *Khudkasht* Peasants

The advantages to the landlord and village that accrued from the *khudkasht* peasant were reflected in the nature of privileges granted to them. Among these was the possibility of enjoying the holding at favourable rent rates, usually fixed by custom. In theory at least, these concessional rents could not be increased. The cultivators could also inherit, mortgage and bequeath their lands and were not evicted as long as they paid their rents. *Khudkasht* peasants had traditionally been exempt from taxes on marriages, or house tax, a fact which reflects their value for the landlord (Chandra 1974). Marriage signalled the possibility of the emergence of a new productive unit as well as gains for the peasant household in the form of the labour of the incoming daughter-in-law. In the ultimate analysis, as the landlord would be a future beneficiary of the ensuing increased productivity, such logic appears to have prompted the exemptions on marriage and house tax granted to *khudkasht* peasant households by landlords in pre-colonial times.

Besides the economic advantages, these peasants could borrow from the village moneylender and avail of other privileges with regard to homestead plots, use of trees, pasture and forest lands, water reservoirs, fisheries and the services of village servants. They had the pick of the fields left unoccupied, and their land was never sold in default of state dues (ibid. 1974). In this sense, as Bhargava (1996) points out for Gorakhpur, *khudkasht* cultivators constituted the village elite, enjoying unchallenged occupancy of the *khudkasht* lands from generation to generation.

Besides the readily available labour of women of *khudkasht* households, other opportunities for surplus accumulation by such households ranged from superior means of production to a permanent interest in the soil they cultivated. These factors ensured autonomy in decision-making with regard to cultivation as well as substantial investments in land. As women's labour while exploited within the family, remains uncompensated, the productive labour of the women of *khudkasht* peasant households was an extension of their domestic duties. The extent of this labour could be unlimited and yet it remained unrecorded. It was the *khudkasht* peasant as head of the household who received the compensation for women's labour in the form of lower rent rates. The degree and extent to which the *khudkasht* households could contribute the labour of their women made for differentiation even within the class of *khudkasht* peasants. This element therefore needs to be incorporated in exercises aimed at assessing the labour exploitation ratio of peasant households as suggested by Utsa Patnaik (1987) in her method for analysing peasant class differentiation.

The privileges of the *khudkasht* peasant when contrasted with those of the *pahikasht*, reveal the hidden role of the women of such households on whose unrecognized labour much of the system of rights and duties seems to have hinged. Yet the invisibility of peasant women in the colonial records is pervasive and their contribution can only be inferred from stray references as offered above. The peasant is constructed as male and it is only through him that *pattas* were issued, rental arrangements made, and *jajmani* relationships entered into.

In contrast to the *khudkasht*, the *pahikasht* peasant did not reside in the village and was thus perceived as having only a temporary interest in the soil. *Pahikasht* peasants moved from place to place in search of better terms which was a hindrance for maintaining their own means of production such as ploughs, bullocks and seed. Nor were the women of *pahikasht* peasants available for cultivation on a regular basis. It was the proprietor or landlord who made the decisions relating to cultivation such as how much to plough, what to sow and how much manure to apply. *Pahikasht* rents were assessed on the basis of *batai*, i.e. on produce and not on a fixed rent-rate. These peasants could bequeath, though not sell or transfer, their holdings. It was however possible for a single cultivator to be a *khudkasht* tenant in one village and a *pahikasht* cultivator in a neighbouring one. Thus these two categories were not always mutually exclusive (Chandra 1974). In Gorakhpur, for instance, Bhargava (1996) points out that the abundance of unoccupied, cultivable lands led the East India Company to offer *pahikasht* cultivators low terms to extend cultivation. This not only encouraged mobility among cultivators but also was an incentive to opt for *pahi* or annual leases on new lands rather than *khudkasht* rights, as well as negotiate for better terms.

Wherever there were more cultivators than land to till, the customary rates paid by *khudkasht* tenants were lower than rates at which a migratory tenant could obtain a holding. As long as plenty of land was available, the *pahi* peasant could bargain or pay *nazrana* and acquire *khudkasht* rights. The position of the *pahis* worsened with increase of pressure on land (Chandra 1974).

Clearly, assumptions about the availability of the labour of able-bodied *khudkasht* peasant family members, including women, determined the structure of rights and privileges of their tenure. In addition, the family's stakes in ensuring maximum productivity and efficiency through the meticulous labour of the peasant women could be strengthened only as long as security of tenure was not in question and was ensured from generation to generation. Where the *khudkasht* peasant also belonged to an industrious cultivating caste such as Koeri, Kurmi, Ahir and Murao, the advantages which accrued to the landlord were further magnified.

Peasant Differentiation : the Caste Factor

In Awadh, peasants were embedded within the caste system, linked by ties of kin and sub-caste community, a majority occupying a position within the agrarian hierarchy and the village community structure determined by birth and fixed for generations. The traditions of the caste and its position within the caste hierarchy further determined the extent to which women's labour within the household could be enlisted for production. Dependence on hired labour increased at the higher rungs of the caste hierarchy, where restrictions on touching the plough were in force. Hired labour was also a necessity where the extent of peasant holdings was considerable or when seasonal requirements demanded extra hands.

An outstanding feature of a large proportion of the cultivating groups in south-eastern Awadh was their ex-proprietary nature. By virtue of being the original settlers they enjoyed the status of proprietors and the rights that went with it. This was a direct consequence of the manner in which the region had been settled by various Rajput clans from the twelfth century onwards. This ex-proprietary status of large sections of cultivators accounted for the differentiation within the class and also the varying degrees of rights enjoyed.[1]

The growth of peasantry in the region may be attributed to the waves of migrations following the Mughal invasions of north India from this time onwards. Fleeing Rajput clans settled in these remote areas of Awadh usually by subjugating the local inhabitants, the earliest of whom appear to have been the tribal Bhars. Another cultivating caste, the Kurmi, claimed to be the earliest inhabitants who were among the first to have cleared the lands, much before the Rajput dominance of the area. The necessity of carrying out basic production for the now dominant Rajputs was fulfilled by the subject population. The status of the vanquished elite was usually recognized for a generation or so, by granting them certain privileges such as revenue-free villages or grazing rights in certain areas. However, over time such rights were obliterated and rendered indistinct. When this happened, even the former ruling groups had little to differentiate them from the common cultivators.[2]

HIGH CASTE PEASANTS

A category of privileged rent-payers, whose rentals were fixed by usage and custom, were the Rajput and Brahmin peasants. Settlement officers after 1857 found the existence of certain *pattas* which had extended over 60 years and which showed that rents had not been raised during this period. The low rents ensured that peasants would not leave their landlords in search of better terms.[3] This consideration is understandable in the case of Rajput peasants who also provided military support to the taluqdars and rajas.

In Awadh, the erstwhile Rajput rajas, many of whom were the taluqdars of the colonial period, had always relied on the support of their subjects against enemies. In colonial times 'taluqdar' was the technical term for landlord who held land by virtue of a document, the *sanad* given by the British government after 1857. To ensure the support, allegiance and respect from peasants, Rajas granted permanent rights in their holdings and did not stretch their demands to the utmost ability to pay. The peasants in turn tilled the rajas' lands, paid dues and provided the fighting men in times of war. As loyalty of subjects was more important than a mere increased receipt of revenue in kind, the peasants' privileges consisted of a right to occupy the land in preference to any other peasant without necessarily involving more favourable terms as regards rent. Although it was very unusual to oust peasants, it was by no means unusual for proprietors to raise rents. The rents were raised to a level that the proprietor was able, depending on his power and influence, to coerce the peasant to pay.[4]

All over Awadh, long possession and belonging to a high caste normally resulted in favour being shown in rents. Even more significant in this context is the fact that caste Brahmin and Rajput peasant women did not work in the fields. Purity taboos dictated that food was cooked and prepared by the women of the household. Within the household, food processing, grinding, etc., was either done by the women themselves or under their supervision by women of serving castes. Today women of high castes often appear in the fields in a supervisory capacity. Traditionally, even the men of these castes safeguarded their prestige and status by not actually using the plough. Given high-caste taboos, a reduction in their rents appears to have been not just an acknowledgement of their caste, but also the allowance for wages of the ploughman.[5] However, it appears that custom in this respect varied from village to village.

The following statements by Rajput peasants recorded at the time of the Settlement when rents were being raised uniformly, reveal their status perceptions and rights enjoyed by them:

> We are men of local repute and influence and if we stood by our landlord no one could hurt him. Our honour was equal to his. We always sat on an equality—we went with him often. Whenever he went on business or pleasure he was received well and when paan was given to him it was given by us. We don't plough with our own hands, *our women do not go outside our houses* (emphasis added). Sweepers do menial work for us. Is our honour less than it was, that the landlord should make us pay rent like Kurmies? Even under Native rule the landlord never raised our rents nor our father or grandfather. We have pattas extending over 60 years to show that we never asked for more than Rs. 2 per bigha. Had he raised our rent we

would have left him and gone to his neighbours and he seeing him to be defenceless, would soon have annexed our village to his taluqa. (Oudh General file 1864-7)[6]

This statement is particularly revealing as it encapsulates the prevalent ideology of high-caste peasants. It expresses pride in the fact that high-caste peasants did not plough themselves; manual labour in the fields, including ploughing, is indicative of low social status. This logic is extended to women so that women's seclusion within the home is an indicator of high social status. Finally the statement is disparaging of all labour and expresses an ideology wherein all manual labour is devalued. Thus on the scale of status and honour, sweepers are regarded the lowest owing to their involvement in menial tasks, Kurmis are placed in the middle of the scale as they are rent-payers, and Rajput peasants head the status hierarchy for their affinity with the landowning caste of the region, the seclusion of women, restrictions on ploughing—all of which get reflected in the lowered rent rates.

Various reasons have been cited for the low rents of Brahmins. Sometimes they appear to be out of consideration for their social position, at others for the religious and other services they rendered, and occasionally as a courtesy accorded to higher castes.[6] As a paradox, while women's labour within the *khudkasht* (resident) peasant household, was the ground for low rents, its unavailability in the case of high-caste peasants did not raise rents. Instead, it was consideration of status that kept rents down. In many parts of Faizabad, high-caste peasants sublet lands to be cultivated by low-caste peasants as their *shikmies* (sub-tenants). The latter were rack-rented freely. On a number of estates, members of Brahmin and Rajput castes held leases of considerable holdings from the superior proprietors to sublet at rack-rents (Jassal 1980). They lived on the difference between the privileged rent rates and rack-rents. *Shikmidars* seldom figured on the rent-rolls.[7]

Changes as a Consequence of Colonial Rule: from Peasant to Tenants-at-will

As in other parts of South Asia, the colonial state forged an alliance with the landed elites, the taluqdars of Awadh, whereby the latter and the underproprietors below them were made sole proprietors of more than 80 per cent of the land. In the Faizabad district during colonial rule, of the 3,601 villages, taluqas or estates included 2,414 or nearly two-thirds of the entire area (Metcalfe 1979). The cultivating peasantry which comprised the majority in the Awadh countryside found itself converted into a class of tenants who held their tenure at the mercy and will of the taluqdars. In its efforts to appease the landed gentry, the colonial state systematically eroded the age-old rights and privileges of Awadh cultivators. In contrast to pre-British times, insecurity of tenure and rack-rents were the characteristic feature of Awadh tenants during colonial rule (Jassal 1988).

In the colonial revenue records, shifting emphasis in nomenclature from local terms to more specific legal categories, is itself indicative of the extent to which traditional age-old rights of cultivators were swept away. The blanket term *kisan* in Awadh was a broad category used in addition to specific local terms such as *khudkasht*, *pahikasht*, *shikmi* which stood for distinct categories of cultivators. For revenue purposes, usages such as 'tenant' and 'landlord' reflected the colonial concern with revenue and allowed for uniformity, unencumbered with the many kinds of rights represented by local terms (ibid.).

Colonial rule struck at some of these privileges while deriving the fullest benefits from the labour of women of *khudkasht* households. Thus, while the colonial state conceded that privileged rent rates fixed by custom should be maintained, the overarching policy of viewing only taluqdars as proprietors, made nonsense of the *khudkasht* tenants' customary ability to inherit, mortgage and bequeath their holdings. *Khudkasht* or resident tenants were now subject to most of the same disadvantages as the other tenants-at-will. The logic of the *khudkasht* tenure, wherein family labour could be enlisted, remained in place to serve the interests of the state and the concessional rent rates recognized and reflected this.

Traditionally it had been commonplace for *khudkasht* tenants to hold more lands than shown in the register, a feature which became increasingly impossible, as stricter controls over the tenantry was demanded of the taluqdars. The latter's own compulsions to meet fixed revenue demands, conflicted with some of the more flexible arrangements *khudkasht* tenants could enter into with their landlords. While the pre-colonial state had valued such a cultivator's capacity to maintain cultivation at a high level and, where necessary and possible, to improve and extend it, the colonial state derived altogether new benefits from the tenure without in any way compensating the *khudkasht* tenant for it. Rather, by ignoring its specificity and subsuming it under the category of tenants-at-will, the state systematically undermined the logic of its existence. The *khudkasht* occupancy rights which were then as prescriptive and hereditary as those of the zamindars, were now confronted with an altered reality in the shape of the Taluqdari Settlement which made arbitrary evictions commonplace and introduced elements of uncertainty in an otherwise secure tenure.

Relegated now to the realm of extra-economic dues and *nazrana* which could be charged by landlords from tenants, the exemptions virtually ceased, while the exact sum which could be charged as tax on marriages and new dwellings varied from taluqa to taluqa, to be fixed arbitrarily by the taluqdar or his estate manager. As *nazrana* payments demanded by taluqdars increased substantially in range and variety, in keeping with the rising revenue demand and altered logic and concerns of the colonial state, the *raison-d'être* for exemptions on tenants' marriages and house tax declined. Rather, these occasions provided landlords with rich possibilities for coercive extractions from tenants. The menace of *nazrana* had reached enormous proportions by the 1920s, and in the lists of *nazranas* charged all over Awadh, house and marriage taxes occupied top slots, offending peasant sensibilities as once these had been significant exemptions meant to reinforce the superior status of *khudkasht* tenants.[8]

The tax exemptions given to *khudkasht* cultivators were indicative of the value of such peasant household units for production. Marriage within the *khudkasht* peasant household meant the creation of a new productive unit and the consequent rise in productivity which was to be encouraged by the exemption from payment of the marriage tax. Consequently this aspect of pre-colonial peasant order characterized by its security and stability was extended to an altered colonial situation with a different logic ruled by maximization of rents, the appropriation of peasant surplus by the state, and a disregard for the cultivator's security of tenure.

Perhaps the most glaring intervention in colonial times which impinged on women's labour within *khudkasht* households and introduced an element of exploitation missing from the pre-colonial arrangements was the injunction on *khudkasht* households not to employ wage labour. The logic was that this would eat into the profits of their households, thereby leaving a greatly reduced portion as the state's share. That the colonial state discouraged *khudkasht* tenants from using hired help for cultivation is evidence of the state's preoccupation with revenue. The state feared that concessional rent rates would allow little or no profit for the state after wages had been paid.

Colonial Impact on Caste

It was state policy as early as 1793, articulated in the Indian Regulation IV, which prompted the colonial state to refrain from interference in the customs and usages of the people. It was thus a political decision to ensure that the private sphere consisting of customs relating to marriage, family, kinship, divorce, inheritance and so on would be regulated by the jati codes. Thus women's position which ensured ranking within the caste hierarchy was to remain untouched by the colonial state, caste distances maintained and strengthened by the legal apparatus of the state. The colonial state laid down that only such customs would be recognized as law which were ancient, observed without interruption, uniform, obligatory and not immoral or opposed to public policy (Roy 1986). These injunctions allowed the state sufficient leeway to intervene even in the sphere of family and customary practices, as and when these conflicted with broader state policies. A case in point is the introduction of compulsory primogeniture for Awadh taluqdars (see Chapter 3). The state's concern with enforcing reduction in marriage expenditures and dowries among landed groups of Awadh, especially as these practices tended to be emulated by upwardly-mobile peasant castes such as the Kurmis, is particularly interesting from the viewpoint of this chapter.[9]

The political and economic calculations of the colonial power are further reflected in its tacit acceptance and endorsement of caste customs that confined women of certain castes (Brahmin, Rajput) to the domestic domain while capitalizing on the labour of women of peasant castes (Ahir, Koeri and Kurmi).[10] Certain arrangements ensured that customary economic practices of distinct peasant groups and peasant castes were unquestioningly enlisted in the service of the state.

In Faizabad, in 1905 low-caste cultivators paid on an average Rs. 5.60 per acre, but Rajput and Brahmin tenants paid Rs. 4.32

per acre (Nevill 1905). As explanation for such glaring inequity in rental of different castes, Jafri argues that certain castes such as Kacchis and Kurmis pay more rent because they make the land yield more, 'the zamindar is anxious to share these larger gains, so these unfortunates are penalised for their good work and their skilled labour brings them little profit' (Jafri 1931: 356).

These divergent positions of the state with regard to caste groups demonstrate that it was adhering to its position of 'non-interference in the customs of the people', where custom among high castes kept women confined to the home (Roy 1986: 23). This brings into focus the larger issue of women's involvement in agricultural production, and the status and caste distinctions within the mass of tenantry which arose from the involvement or otherwise of women in productive labour. Hence to see tenants of Faizabad as homogeneous, obscures the reality.

In 1875, only 18 per cent of the Faizabad population was composed of high-caste tenants. Under the changed circumstances of colonial rule, the privileged rent rates of high-caste tenants and status restrictions on women working in fields, began to be regarded as a distinct liability by landlords. As a result, notices for eviction issued to high-caste tenants by taluqdars increased considerably during this period. The phenomenon was reported in most taluqas where sizeable concentrations of high-caste tenants were found. Table 5 indicates the number of eviction notices issued in Faizabad in 1875.[11]

As indicated by the figures in Table 5, the notices issued to both Brahmin and Rajput tenants combined, 1,520 in all, exceeded those

TABLE 5: STATEMENT SHOWING NOTICES OF EJECTMENT IN FAIZABAD IN 1875

Name of tehsil	*No. of villages in tehsil*	*No. of villages in which notices issued*	*No. of notices issued to*			
			Brahmins	*Rajputs*	*Others*	*Total*
Faizabad	493	129	157	160	268	585
Bikapur	631	180	161	251	113	525
Akbarpur	665	158	146	143	204	493
Tanda	1,034	262	340	162	439	941
Total	2,823	729	804	716	1,024	2,544

Source: Oudh General file 1341, part III, p. 146.

issued to all other castes together (1024). This is significant as only 18 per cent of the population was composed of these two castes. The preponderance of notices to the two high castes is attributed to the belief that tenants of these castes were the worst cultivators, prone to paying their rents less readily than low-caste tenants, in spite of their lower rent rates.

Commissioner Capper, to whom most of these cases went in appeal, reported that he could seldom trace enmity as the reason. He found that tenants evicted were frequently from high castes, well-to-do, and those who had managed to secure some of the best lands in the village and on some pretext had continually avoided payment of even the light rent which was agreed.[12] On the other hand, according to Capper, notices of eviction were seldom issued against Kacchis, Muraos and Kurmis, cultivating castes known for their industry and agricultural skills, whose women carried out a range of agricultural operations alongside the men and who could be called upon to do forced labour.[13]

Thus whereas high-caste cultivators, especially Rajputs, had been favoured by Rajput landlords in the past for the military support and security provided to the erstwhile petty rajas/taluqdars through sheer strength of their numbers, Brahmin peasants offered an element of prestige. These considerations under the altered circumstances of colonial rule were seen as luxuries few taluqas could afford, as functions of this sort were rendered obsolete, with the state making its own provisions for militia and police. Low rents fixed by custom meant long-term inability on the part of taluqdars to meet state revenue demands as well as lowered agricultural productivity largely resulting from high-caste women's exclusion from agricultural production. With its emphasis on improved productivity combined with high revenues, the state's new 'improving landlords', the taluqdars, made concerted efforts to evict such tenants and encouraged peasant castes from the middle rungs of the caste hierarchy to settle on their estates. Elsewhere I have shown that significantly, even factors such as kinship and caste ties did little to mitigate taluqdars' resolve to issue ejection notices to high caste tenants wherever they proved to be recalcitrant (Jassal 1980: 323-6).

The insecurity of tenure of Awadh tenants soon became well-known in the districts of the Benaras Division which bordered Awadh. The scale of eviction among Kewats and Koeris had an impact on the forging of affinal ties and marriage alliances within caste members settled in neighbouring districts. It was noted that cultivating castes were unable to find brides from neighbouring Jaunpur district as fathers were wary of giving daughters in marriage 'to someone who is a Rais today who may become a beggar tomorrow'.[14] This observation is indicative of the extent of disenchantment in the countryside with colonial rule which had introduced the phenomenon of arbitrary eviction among peasant castes known for their industry and skill.

Growth in *Begar*

It is in the realm of forced labour that kisan women's wide-ranging contributions in the rural economy can be estimated. Theoretically, both men and women of an average cultivator's household could be summoned by the landlord to do *begari* on his land usually in the months of *Asarh* and *Kartik*, i.e. twice a year. Customarily, these duties included ploughing, assisting in the transplantation of rice, or working on the basket lifts for *rabi* irrigation. In return for such labour, the payment was parched grain for half a day's work and 2 *seers* of grain for a day's work (Nevill 1905: 52). In the period from 1870 to the 1920s, *begari* became increasingly common, particularly on the lands of smaller zamindars, especially of coparcenary holdings.

On an average, tenants-at-will were found to be contributing their labour for the landlord's farm once in every eight days.[15] In Faizabad, Brahmins and Rajputs appear to have been exempt from the service dues while the Chamars were most exploited. Chamars often ended up working two to five days per week, carrying articles as porters or cutting wood for the landlord without payment. In Faizabad district, village *pattidars* or holders of shares in coparcenary holdings, enlisted for *begari* the women of kisan households settled on their lands. Pounding and grinding the grain of the *malik* (overlord) was an inescapable task for most women, often accompanied by threats and coercion, a fact discussed at length by Baba Ramchandra, a prominent peasant leader of the region who successfully mobilized the Awadh peasantry during the 1920s and 1930s. Kumar mentions a petition from the 1930s entitled, *Anath Ablaon Ki Pukar* (Demands of Helpless Women). It was penned by Baba Ramchandra on behalf of women, and five of their major grievances were listed. These were:

(a) We are beaten with lathis,
(b) Being forced to stand on a mudpot in the glaring sun we are watched with lustful eyes,
(c) During begar they make us grind. If we refuse, we are beaten with lathis. They break our heads,
(d) After the death of our husbands we are evicted from our holdings, houses, orchards, etc.,
(e) Thus we cannot repay loans nor manage our family (*Baba Ramchandra Papers*. Serial File no. 4, also quoted in Kumar 1989: 360).

Other evidence pertains to the consequences for women of refusal to provide labour. Refusal could incite landlords to enter peasant homes, insult, and on occasion rain blows on the women. There are innumerable references to *maliks* entering homes and walking off with household articles.[16] Clearly, much of this labour could only be forcibly extracted, which suggests that the legitimacy for labour demands of this kind had already eroded in peasant perceptions.

The peculiarities of under proprietary tenures in Faizabad as well as the presence of smaller zamindars who held their rights under the taluqdars, made for a complex structure where kisans often owed loyalty to more than one malik. Where zamindari holdings were shared among four or five separate *hissedars*, each peasant served four or five maliks and consequently was expected to be available for any or all of them before he could work on his own fields.[17] What complicated the situation further was that small zamindars were inadequately equipped with bullocks, ploughs and seeds—all of which had to be liberally borrowed. Ironically, zamindars claimed rights over the use of these means of cultivation possessed by the peasant households settled on their lands. As there was acute pressure on the use of these items during the sowing season, tenants were faced with delays in sowing their own fields. Similarly ponds, *jhils* and wells were harnessed to first irrigate the landlord's self-cultivated holdings. Baba Ramchandra's writings draw attention to the plight of tenants whose rents were never pardoned despite delays caused in this manner. Notwithstanding the delays, tenants appear to have been under considerable pressure to pay up every paise of the rent.[18]

CONCLUSION

In my analysis of the peasantry in colonial Awadh I have attempted to shift the focus to the nature of women's productive activity and its utilization in agrarian production as significant factors in increasing differentiation within the peasantry. The hypothesis explored is the extent to which differentiation between classes is dependent upon and centres around the utilization of women's productivity, as the latter is also a yardstick of distinctions of rank and status. While participation in production may signify access to productive resources and a considerable degree of gender equality, this by no means ensures a high position in the status/class hierarchy. Rather there seems to be an inverse relationship between the two. The evidence from among the Faizabad tenantry indicates that two processes were at work simultaneously, which affected both upper-caste and lower-caste/class women in different ways, leading to the subordination of women of both categories. These processes may be identified as:

(a) the exploitation of the labour of women from the *khudkast*, middle and lower peasant castes to generate surpluses,
(b) the traditional unavailability of upper-caste peasant women for direct participation in production.

In the first category women had no control over the products of their labour which was appropriated by the proprietary classes, taluqdars and zamindars. In the second, the traditional withdrawal from productive resources, while indicative of the higher status of the peasant household, did not signify major advantages for its women, except for privileges such as greater social security and leisure.

Thus one finds that peasant women of both categories experienced powerlessness which was a consequence of the lack of access to resources. This was further manifested in a devaluation of the work that women did. Middle- and low-caste peasant women of Faizabad also lacked control over their own labour, time, and skills. Their acute vulnerability was evident in the practice of *begari* and their subjection to violence at the hands of landlords. This exercise in understanding peasant differentiation through a re-reading of the historical evidence, with a focus on women's roles in agrarian production, is also an attempt at redressing the overwhelming male bias in agrarian studies. My emphasis therefore is only a small beginning towards a more comprehensive and holistic analysis of socio-historical processes.

The next chapter engages with the women of the proprietary class, that of the taluqdars of Awadh, who held 80 per cent of the land in the region. The picture of rural Awadh would be incomplete without a discussion of women of the rent-receiving class. As women of the landed elite, their seclusion from agricultural activities affected them differently compared to the women discussed earlier.

NOTES

*This chapter is a modified version of a paper which appeared under the title 'Hidden Peasant Women in Colonial Awadh', *Indian Journal of Gender Studies*, vol. 5, no. 1, Jan.-June 1998: 1-22.

1. Oudh General file 1804, 1864-7. Record of Rights of Ex-proprietary Cultivators on Taluqdari Estates, U.P. State Archives, Lucknow.
2. Ibid.
3. Oudh General file 1951, 1867-8. U.P. State Archives, Lucknow.
4. Oudh General file 2182, U.P. State Archives, Lucknow.
5. Oudh General file 1867-8.
6. Oudh General file 2182.
7. Oudh General file 1883.
8. Oudh General file 1864-7: 245.
9. Foreign Dept. General Branch, 28. Consultation 1864. On the Alleged Curtailment of Marriage Expenses Among Rajputs. National Archives, New Delhi.
10. Oudh General file 394. Enquiry into the Condition of Tenantry in Oudh. U.P. State Archives, Lucknow.
11. Oudh General file 1341, part 3: 146. U.P. State Archives, Lucknow.
12. Oudh General file 1942, part 3. U.P. State Archives.
13. Oudh General file 1010, 1881-2. Relations of Landlords and Tenants in North India. U.P. State Archives, Lucknow.
14. Mehta Report, Exhibit S, file 753/1920. Revenue 'A', p. 89. U.P. State Archives, Lucknow.
15. *Baba Ramchandra Papers*, Ist Instalment , file 3. Nehru Memorial Museum & Library, New Delhi.
16. Ibid.
17. Ibid.
18. *Baba Ramchandra Papers, 1933-50*, Nehru Memorial Museum & Library, New Delhi.

CHAPTER 3

Custom, Legislation and Landownership: Where are the Women?

> A critical knowledge of the evolution of the idea of property would embody, in some respects, the most remarkable portion of the mental history of mankind.
>
> L.H. Morgan, 1877, *Ancient Society*, p. 6, cited in V.G. Kiernan, 'Private Property in History', in J. Goody, J. Thirsk and E.P. Thompson (eds.), 1976, *Family and Inheritance*, Cambridge: Cambridge University Press (361)

> Primogenitural succession and proprietary impartibility are important diagnostics of the rise of the raja.
>
> R.G. Fox, 1971, *Kin, Clan, Raja and Rule*, Bombay: Oxford University Press (49)

> In an extreme case, in the early twentieth century, the dowager Maharani of the Ayodhya (Mehdona) estate daily cooked her own meals for fear of being poisoned by the manager. Until the taluqdar's death this individual had enjoyed the complete trust of his employer.
>
> S.T. Jassal, 1988, 'Agrarian Structure: A Study of the Faizabad District', unpublished Ph.D. thesis, Dept. of Sociology, Delhi University

The manner in which regional agrarian structures have been shaped by a variety of colonial interventions has received widespread scholarly attention. Scholars have explored the impact of legal measures on regional agrarian structures and the processes of change that were unleashed. The colonial experiment in Awadh, which began after its annexation in 1856, is representative of land settlements initiated to create a landed gentry which could act as the bulwark of colonial rule but which in turn gave rise to transformative social processes that affected all classes and vastly restructured society. In Awadh, the experiment with the taluqdars is of particular interest for the way in which relations between taluqdars and the peasants were altered. Known for peasant resistance and the spontaneous peasant uprisings of the 1920s, Awadh's history starting from the Mutiny onwards, has been one of increasing volatility and steadily deteriorating agrarian relations. Somewhat less researched is the long-term impact of individual legislations on the target group or class for which they were intended. Focusing on gender differentiation within one class, that comprising the owners of estates, the non-cultivating taluqdars, this chapter seeks to chart a relatively less-known terrain. While what constitutes a class may be seen only against other classes in the agrarian structure, such a focus is also likely to exclude analysis of conflicting interests within classes, including gender-based ones. Assumptions of gender parity in the impact of legislations have hitherto clouded understanding of agrarian change. Located within an ongoing debate on the nature of the colonial state, this chapter is aimed as a step forward in the understanding of the actual workings of concrete legislations with long-term effects on social groups.

My point of departure is the legislative impact on an agrarian structure located within defined geographical limits and of a particular period. With special focus on the Awadh Taluqdari Succession Act of 1869, I analyse court and archival data from the Faizabad district covering the period from 1869 to the 1920s. In subjecting the historical and empirical evidence to closer scrutiny, I propose to highlight both the intended and unintended consequences of the legislation, particularly for women. Did the Act represent a complete rupture, or was it a modification of existing tendencies? To what extent was the flexibility of traditions and customs eroded, and what were the strains created in the process? In this sense, what were the continuities and breaks with the past?

The Taluqdari Succession Act of 1869 allows for an exploration of the distinct and stated advantages conferred on the taluqdars as well as the corresponding disadvantages it spelt for women of taluqdari or proprietary families of Awadh. My focus allows for investigating whether membership in the most privileged class in the agrarian structure necessarily conferred economic privileges on the women of that class. What is the nature of privileges that accrue to women and how do these differ from those enjoyed by men? In terms of ownership and control over resources, what are the advantages enjoyed by women? As regards the autonomy of women one needs to investigate the sources of power within the extended family. How does lack of ownership or lack of direct control of land translate into lack of autonomy in decision-making and accompanying powerlessness? Finally, how did a colonial legislation freeze the existing possibilities of ownership, control and autonomy existing within the system of customs and traditions?

The social implications of the Taluqdari Succession Act of 1869 are immense, as adherence to primogeniture in inheritance was made compulsory for all taluqdari families. As early as 1793, the colonial state through the Indian Regulation IV had asserted its commitment to non-interference in the customs and usages of the people. Inheritance, marriage, rights to succession, religious endowments, adoption, etc., had always been included under Hindu or Muslim personal law, or governed by the religious customs of the two communities (Roy 1986). In Awadh, the combination of political and administrative exigencies and colonial policy led to the sacrifice of the sanctity of custom in favour of primogeniture for taluqdars of both Hindu and Muslim families. Being directly in opposition to the state's proclaimed 'hands off' policy on the vital issue of customary law, the working of the Act affords insights into the way in which law interfaces with local custom.

Under colonial rule introduced in Awadh after annexation in 1856, taluqdars came to be defined as proprietors of landed estates or taluqas, and responsible for the state's revenues from their estates. The Taluqdari Succession Act or Act I of 1869, passed a decade after annexation, represents one among a series of arrangements made with regional ruling elites to secure legitimacy for colonial rule. As the support and loyalty of this influential elite was seen as a political necessity, taluqdars were befriended and legislations passed to ensure that taluqas would remain intact in perpetuity—this was in turn necessitated by the fact that many Hindu and Muslim taluqdars practised partible inheritance.

Since 'intentions in inheritance systems as in other matters eventuate in conclusions very different from those intended' (Thompson 1976: 328), the functioning of the Act over a period of approximately half a century, affords the possibility of apprehending the process overtime. The ramifications of the Act were seen in the economy and polity, and also in kinship structure and marriage practice. While women had been proprietors of estates, though only under severely restricted conditions, I explore how the ideology of primogeniture meant a step backward for them. Hence the scope of the chapter includes the further deterioration in the status of taluqdari women, arising from continued disabilities and exclusion from ownership and control of taluqas.

COLONIAL POLICY AND TALUQDARI RIGHTS

The Taluqdari Succession Act of 1869 was an important component of the 'Oudh Policy' which informed the entire period of British rule in Awadh (Metcalf 1979). The events of the Mutiny prompted the urgent search for loyal political allies who could be counted on to support the colonial state as well as ensure order and stability in the region. Identified as the 'natural leaders' most liable to fulfil these requirements, the taluqdars became the focus of the Oudh Policy. The alliance was marked by a process of definition and delimitation of the class of taluqdars to form an exclusive and rigidly-defined group. The term taluqdar now acquired a precise legal meaning.

As only those opulent landholders paying Rs. 5,000 or above as revenue were included in the definition of taluqdars, several holders of long-established estates found themselves reduced in status.[1] When the rights of these underproprietors were recognized and recorded, it was under the dominance and dependence of the taluqdars. Hence, what was once a continuum which included taluqdars of varying degrees of economic strength, now became a class with its boundaries closed for all time. Individuals of diverse backgrounds ranging from erstwhile rajas of small principalities to more recent revenue-farmers of Mughal times, with demonstrated loyalty to the British during the Mutiny, were included in this class. Hence, some taluqdars traced their origins to ruling lineages established in the eleventh and twelfth century. Rajput kingdoms which had emerged in the wake of Muslim invasions in the north, while others were of more recent origin, referred to as 'mushroom taluqdars', having risen to power and acquired taluqas as revenue functionaries and tax farmers during the Nawabi (Nevill 1905). The diverse composition of this class in terms of origins is significant in apprehending the differential impact of the Act.

On conclusion of the Settlement process, 80 per cent of Faizabad's entire land came under the proprietary possession of only 26 taluqdars, while in the Awadh province with its 12 districts, the number of taluqdars amounted to 276. In the Faizabad district, of the 3,601 villages, taluqas or estates included 2,414 villages or nearly two-thirds of the entire area (Millett 1880). Out of the 26 taluqdars, 17 were Hindus and nine Muslims. Among the Hindus, 15 were Rajputs belonging to four clans, Rajkumar, Bachgoti, Palwer and Gargbansi. Among the Muslims, three belonged to Muslim Bachgoti Rajput and four to Saiyyid. The former were genealogically related to the Bachgoti Rajputs and were called Khanzadas after conversion (Nevill 1905).

Taluqdars were responsible to the government for the payment of fixed revenue demands from their estates. This was in turn realized in the form of rents from tenants (Metcalf 1979). Rents were realized in cash though the appropriation of agricultural surplus also took the form of rents in kind, forced labour and various kinds of taxes and cesses.[2]

The irreversibility of the process of definition was ensured by the issuing of *sanads* which spelt out the rights and duties of taluqdars. It needs to be stressed that the *sanads* granted full proprietary, heritable, alienable and transferable rights in their taluqas. The *sanads* also conveyed explicit assurances from the governor-general and viceroy, confirming the taluqdars in full proprietary possession of their estates and granting them the privilege of engaging directly with the government for the revenue collection from their estates.[3]

The system of layered rights on the same piece of land which characterized the Indian context, thus stood challenged and altered by the new settlement. As already mentioned, it soon dawned on the policy-makers that taluqas were unlikely to remain intact unless propped up by compulsory primogeniture in inheritance. And 'the unlimited power of disposing of their estates given to Talookdars by their sunnuds must lead to the extinction of a landed aristocracy, besides generating bitter feuds and bad blood'.[4]

Correspondence between administrators on the subject of the proposed legislation expressed concern that subdivision of holdings would lead to the extinction of a large majority of landed proprietors or 'unjust and capricious alienation to families of strange blood, which would cause a disruption of all the old traditions and associations that connect a landed aristocracy with the other classes of the rural population, and would rob it of most of its social and political usefulness'.[5] Even more unwanted would be the passing of the great Bais Sombunsee and Bachgoti estates to a new class of landholders who would 'fail to secure the attachment of the population of their estates' and, 'instead of conducing to the good government and prosperity of the province, they would become a source of dissensions and disquiet'.[6]

The Act of 1869 was therefore an immediate response to the situation on the ground while the issuing of *sanads* was motivated by political concerns enshrined in an overarching Oudh Policy. As it has been seen, the Act represented a reversal of an earlier policy relating to non-interference into the personal laws of the people, yet derived its justification from the purported fulfilment of immediate state needs. Furthermore, even as a response to an immediate state requirement, the Act stands in striking contrast with neighbouring Punjab, where an altogether different measure was adopted, pointing to the diverse approaches directed towards achievement of similar goals.

The search for political allies in Punjab led to arrangements wherein the state forged alliances with the heads of extended clan-based kin groups (Gilmartin 1981: 152). Here it was in the state's interest to support a system of law which would preserve the 'tribal' structure of society. The Punjab Laws Act 1872 laid down that

> all questions regarding succession, female's special property, betrothal, dower, adoption, guardianship, minority, custody, family relations, wills, legacies, gifts, partition, religious institutions and alluvion and diluvion are to be settled according to the custom prevailing in the first instance and where no custom exists, the personal laws of the parties must be applied. (ibid.)

Thus, while in Punjab the political purpose of the state was served by a commitment to upholding custom, in Awadh legislation explicitly overruled custom and usage.

FAIZABAD TALUQDARS: RELIGIOUS, CASTE AND CLAN ORIGINS

Legends and genealogies which were often fictive, and legitimized the political power wielded by ruling clans, linked several of the Awadh taluqdars to the Rajput princely lineages of Rajasthan. A large number of Faizabad taluqdars traced their ancestry to a common ancestor, Barriar Singh, a Chauhan Rajput who migrated to Sultanpur in the late thirteenth century from Mainpuri district and the region known as the middle Doab.

Among the Rajput clans who converted to Islam, was that of the Raja of Hasanpur whose descendants came to be known as Khanzadas. The Raja was a Bachgoti Rajput claiming descent from Barriar Singh, like the other Rajput Bachgoti and Rajkumar clans. Later the chieftains of Dera, Meopur and Kurwar estates also followed in his footsteps. The Khanzadas retained the customs of the Rajputs and the respect of their kinsmen. The Muslim Bachgoti raja of Hasanpur had been empowered by the sixteenth century ruler Sher Shah Sur to invest with the *tilak* all the rajas of south-eastern Awadh. This information becomes significant in the light of the fact that from the sixteenth century onwards, no succession to a kingdom was recognized as valid without an award by the emperor to his representative. The investiture ceremony took the form of a gathering of the raja's kinsmen and leading chiefs of the neighbourhood, who by their presence testified to his legitimacy. The *tilak* was the royal insignia on a new raja's forehead (Millett 1880: 124).

Until as late as the 1930s, the Khanzadas performed their marriage ceremonies according to Rajput customs, to the extent of consulting the Nai and Brahmin. Divorce and widow remarriage began making inroads around the 1930s. *Mundan* (tonsure of babies) and *chathi* (the sixth day after birth) ceremonies were observed according to Rajput tradition. But burial of the dead was according to Islamic rites. Women worshipped Sitla and other Hindu gods and goddesses and prohibitions with regard to smoking and eating with low-caste Muslims were observed (Census 1931). These observations parallel those of Ibbetson (1881) from Punjab, noting that despite conversion to Islam, Muslim Rajputs had not eschewed their former customs and practices. It appears that conversion for strategic reasons did not greatly diminish the standing of ruling clans, particularly with regard to marriage alliances.

THE TALUQDARI SUCCESSION ACT OF 1869

By the Taluqdari Succession Act of 1869, the eldest son was to be the successor of a taluqdari estate, the assumption being that the landlord community could flourish in Awadh only by adhering to the laws of property which had given rise to such a gentry in Britain (Metcalf 1979). In case of intestacy, the estate was to devolve upon the eldest son, failing which it went to the senior-most living son, then to the heir by adoption and then to the nearest collateral male heir. In default of all these, the estate passed to a widow for life and on her death, to a male child whom she may choose to adopt (Lal 1942). The exact order of preference was therefore as follows:

1. The eldest son and his male lineal descendants;
2. If the eldest son died during the taluqdar's lifetime leaving male lineal descendants, then to the eldest and every other son of such eldest son, successively, according to their respective seniorities and the respective male lineal descendants;
3. If the eldest son died without leaving male descendants, then the second and every other son of the taluqdar;
4. In default of the above, the estate devolved on the adopted children of the taluqdar;
5. In the absence of the adopted son and his lineal descendants, to the eldest and every other brother of the taluqdar.
6. In default of such brother or his male lineal descendants, to the widow of the deceased taluqdar, only for her lifetime—a senior widow being preferred to a junior one.
7. On the death of such a widow, to such son as the widow should with consent (in writing) of her deceased husband have adopted.
8. In default of these, the next widow in order of seniority.
9. In default of these, the mother of the deceased taluqdar and for her lifetime only.
10. In default or on death of such a mother, the nearest male agnate;
11. In default of any such agnate, to such person as would have been entitled to succeed to the estate under the ordinary law to which persons of the religion and tribe of the taluqdar are subject (*Babu Achai Singh* vs. *Babuain Shangunath Koer*, Oudh Cases, 1924, vol. 28).

In the following section I shall attempt a brief overview of the history of primogeniture in Awadh and the various built-in mechanisms which appear to have contained the inherent tensions arising from hereditary succession.

PRIMOGENITURE: TRADITIONS AND HISTORY

In order to comprehend the extent to which the Taluqdari Succession Act may have represented, in a limited way, a continuity of particular customs and traditions, at least among the ancient princely families while representing a radical change from the past for other taluqdars, it is important to consider the history of primogeniture in Awadh. It is only within this context that the long-term impact of the legislation during the colonial period can be assessed. In addition, as there were subtle customary regional, family and clan variations in inheritance and succession practices which were nevertheless subsumed under the term, this discussion throws into sharper relief the changes introduced by the Act.

All over north India, primogeniture appears to have been known as the '*gaddee*' (throne or seat) principle and its spread was considerable at least among Rajput ruling families, including those of Awadh. In Rajasthan, central India and large areas of the NWP and Awadh, inheritance to Rajput states and to *thinkanas* (estates) was primarily by primogeniture. However, *gaddee* was only one among the wide range of customary laws relating to inheritance and succession.

Plunkett draws attention to the internal stratification within Rajputs themselves, suggesting that observance of primogeniture distinguished the elite and noble clans of a region from the commoner Rajputs (Plunkett 1973: 64). In Awadh, owing to the diverse origins of taluqdars, primogeniture was familiar only to those among them who traced ancient Rajput origins, but relatively unknown among recent 'mushroom taluqdars' of the Nawabi. Even among the ancient clans, for various historical reasons as it will be shown, not all in fact observed primogeniture.

An enquiry ostensibly undertaken as preliminary groundwork for the passing of the Act, placed at the modest figure of 30 the number of families actually observing the *gaddee* custom at Awadh's annexation in 1856. It was these families in the entire Awadh region which were identified as practising the system whereby estates devolved on a single heir according to custom.[7] Moreover, according to the survey, where *gaddee* was the rule the strongest and most able son appears to have often inherited the estate rather than the eldest son.[8]

This finding appears to parallel Brara's observations with regard to Muslim royalty. She points out that among Muslims, fraternal succession as well as primogeniture were prevalent and that 'the fittest rather than the eldest son usually succeeded to his father's throne' (Brara 1994: 138). Based on extensive research among the ruling clans of Rajasthan, Tod arrived at similar conclusions, drawing attention to several instances of attempts by rulers to designate heirs who may not necessarily be eldest sons. This appears to have triggered disputes amongst collaterals on the occasion of succession, with ranis invariably playing significant roles in such struggles (Tod 1832 [1983]).

If inheritance and succession procedures among ruling clans are observed over several generations, as Fox has done for Awadh and Brara for the Malerkotla chiefdom, a pattern seems to emerge where both partible and impartible forms may be adopted, in keeping with the ruling lineage's changing relations with the central political authority. Fox points to the flexibility with which Rajput lineages started out with partible inheritance, then adopted primogeniture and impartible inheritance at some stage in their development, reverting again thereafter to partible forms (Fox 1971: 81). According to Fox this reality precludes the understanding of succession to the *gaddee* in terms of an inviolable jural or ideological principle. Perceptive Awadh administrators observed, 'the stronger the pressure from outside, the more have the clan cohered to resist it: and no doubt to the instinct of self-preservation may be traced much of the vitality which distinguishes them'.[9]

Similarly, Muslim Sherwani chiefs of the Malerkotla kingdom appear to have observed fraternal succession, but when the imperial power waned, Malerkotla veered towards becoming an impartible powerful *riyasat* state (Brara 1994: 215). These insights suggest a continuum with the exclusive unitary principle characteristic of primogeniture at one end and the principle of shared partible and equal inheritance among collaterals on the other. The tension between primogeniture and fraternal succession to chiefship was thus characteristic of a political order based on hereditary rule. Lyall thus summarizes Rajput polity: 'there was a constant struggle between the ordinary rule of Hindu succession to property which divides off the land among the sons at each succession and the rule of political expediency which inclines towards primogeniture' (Lyall 1884: 217). Even where political compulsions necessitated impartibility of estates, the chief though eldest, was after all only the first among equals—the cause of the inherent tension built ino the situation. Hence the prevailing ideology in such circumstances allowed for the sharing of other prerogatives of rulers among collaterals (Brara 1994: 218). To provide military support and unstinted loyalty to the raja, the younger siblings would thus appear to have had similar stakes in the continuance of the *gaddee* or chiefship. Echoes of these sentiments are heard in the evidence from Awadh when the settlement with the taluqdars was perceived by them as leaving out of the equation with the British, the collaterals' significant role, historical contribution and noble status.

ROLE OF AFFINITY AND NATURE OF ALLIANCES AMONG RULING CLANS

Apart from descent, the role of filiation among Rajput ruling clans had significant implications for pre-colonial primogeniture, as political alliances were forged through appropriate marriages. A tendency among ruling Rajputs to enter into multiple marriages until well ino the twentieth century is a significant point made by Tod in this connection. He discusses the consequences of this for the observance of strict primogeniture: the rivalries between queens and the large numbers of sons who had to be provided for.

A case which came to the notice of the chief commissioner of Awadh, was that of the raja of Hasanpur, the head of the Bachgoti clan, who had acknowledged as his son the offspring of a courtesan. The boy was born even before the courtesan became acquainted with the raja. Rajput taluqdars of eastern Awadh were reported to be incensed and sought the intervention of the chief commissioner.

The latter informed the raja that the government would never recognize this 'son' as the heir to the estate, but would support the rights of his brother as his successor. However, the taluqdar declared the courtesan's son as heir. In opposing the move, the chief commissioner was conscious that 'every taluqdar in Oudh would have felt aggrieved that a dishonour had been done to his race, which he would have blamed the government for having permitted'.[10]

Plunkett points to the political advantages of alliances secured by a ruler contracting a first marriage for purposes of providing a suitable successor, and subsequent ones for furthering political gains. Whatever the number of marriages, Plunkett suggests that 'formal status in the "zenana" was reserved for the wife married first and to the mother of the first born son, regardless of their origins' (Plunkett 1973: 66).

Plunkett also refutes Dumont's thesis with reference to formal differentiation among sons of different mothers according to the mother's status, contrary evidence to which is seen in at least one case from Awadh. Husain Baksh who had several wives appointed the offspring of his '*zaujabyahta*', the first or principal wife as the inheritor of the estate. In accordance with the custom of this family, the offspring of the inferior or '*nikahi* wives' were given a single village each for their maintenance (*Nazir Ahmed* vs. *Swami Dayal*, Oudh Cases, 1911). The family customs of the communities sometimes appear to have made provisions for a taluqdar's offspring, depending on the status of the mother. In this case, Husain Baksh gifted his entire property during his lifetime to his two sons from the senior wife in the proportion of 9/16 to the elder and 7/16 to the younger son, thereby disinheriting his wife and two daughters. Not only was this contrary to Hanafi law, but also overlooked family customs whereby the offspring of inferior wives did have to be provided for. (Under Muslim law if the entire estate was treated as a unit of 16 *annas*, then the first wife Munni Begam, should have succeeded to a share of 2 *annas*, the two sons to a share of 4 *annas* 8 *pies* each, and the two daughters to a share of 2 *annas* 4 *pies* each. The case came to court when the son of one of the daughters claimed his share of 1 *anna* 11$^{1}/_{3}$ *pies* out of the 2 *annas* 4 *pies* to be inherited by his mother, the taluqdar's daughter.)

In contrast with the customs of Rajput and Muslim ruling clans, one finds that a Kayastha taluqdar's family traditions contained in the *Wajib-ul-arz* of the village Khanpur, were even more explicit in terms of the way property was to be divided among sons from a number of wives. If there were several wedded wives and sons in varying numbers from each of them, inheritance was to be divided with reference to the number of wives according to the *jurabant* principle which worked as follows: (1) If a wife has only one son, he will take possession of one-half-share of the deceased's inheritance. (2) Where the remaining wife has more than one son, all such sons would take possession of the remaining half of the deceased's inheritance. (3) If some wives have sons and others do not, then each wife as has no sons, shall take shares for their lifetimes and after the death of such wives, the sons of the other wives will be 'malik' of such shares. (4) If none of the wives has sons, the wives of the deceased shall become malik over the inheritance of the deceased in equal shares (Oudh Cases, vol. XXIX, no. 73, 1924: 153).

On one estate there was a family custom whereby the reigning raja was expected to appoint a *yuvraj* to succeed him on his death and a previously appointed *burra thakur* who would succeed in case the *yuvraj* died. In 1813, a raja's widow claimed an estate on the grounds that the raja had not appointed a *yuvraj*. However, as the raja had succeeded in appointing a *burra thakur* before he died, the claims of this individual were seen as stronger than those of the widow and the former succeeded to the *gaddee* (Roy 1908: 46-51).

The above customs are indicative of the variety of arrangements made for collaterals and the claims of sons that may arise from multiple wives, even where primogeniture was practised. They highlight the flexibility of customary laws which had evolved as built-in mechanisms for ensuring amicable settlements so that tensions ensuing from inheritance and succession would not threaten social stability.

In keeping with the north Indian injunctions on caste endogamy and clan exogamy, Rajput clans practised hypergamy whereby daughters were invariably married into clans higher than their natal clan while brides for sons could be accepted from clans of inferior social status. Thus wife-givers were always distinguished from wife-takers. Through this system of marriage alliances, Rajput clans of Faizabad were affinally linked to ruling clans as far away as Rajputana, Mainpuri and Rewa in the west, and Gorakhpur in the east, and such affines were regarded as political allies.

For instance, the Bachgotis gave their daughters to the following clans: Surajbansis, Sombansis, Sirnet, Kalhans, Kanhpuriya, Tilokchandi Bais and Bandhalgoti clans and received wives from the Gargbansis, Raghubansis, Kath Bais, Bhale Sultans, Surwar, Raikwar, Palwer, Nikumbh, Dirgbansis, Chaupat Khambh, Tesahiya and Bilkhariya (Bahadur 1978: 37). The Chauhans of Awadh gave daughters to Bisen, Bandalghoti, Bhale Sultan, Bais, Raikwar, Gauh, Surajbans, Kalhans and Barheiliya They received wives from Kath Bais, Ahban, Palwer and Rathor clans (ibid.: 65). The Palwars gave daughters to Rajkumar, Rajwar, Bachgoti, Gargbansi, Kanhpuriya, Bhale Sultan, Surajbansi, Sombansi and Raghubansi and took wives from Nikumbh, Donwar, Barwar, Chandel, Raghubansi and Bais (ibid.: 114). Thus, the distinction between wife-givers and wife-takers was maintained and was a significant indicator of the clan's position within the Rajput clan status hierarchy.

Brara's comments regarding affinal and maternal relatives outside the *jagir* buttressing the chief's position against collaterals in Malerkotla point to an interesting line of enquiry. She suggests that 'On having once married a daughter to the chief at Malerkotla, marriages of other daughters of the wife-giving lineage to the chief's collaterals and descendants sometimes followed' (Brara 1979: 224). Indeed, the generational links established between Rajput clans point to this possibility. Certainly there is evidence from Faizabad of marriage festivities involving more than one pair of brides and grooms from the wife-giving and wife-taking groups.[11]

Variations in primogeniture appear to have been known to a range of ruling families in European history (Goody 1976: 1-36) There is also sufficient evidence to refute the commonly held view that primogeniture invariably excluded females. Cooper cites evidence to show that it was possible for widows to inherit, though males of remoter degree took precedence over females (Cooper 1976: 199). Plunkett and Tod cite evidence that despite seclusion, Rajput wives often controlled property: that land grants provided for their maintenance, and that wives exercised considerable influence on affairs of state. Ranis also used their resources and connections to wield power and in cases of intestacy, were consulted on choices of collaterals as successors. Usually the collateral was then adopted by the senior rani. Further, as regents for minor sons until they came of age, ranis appear to have played important roles (Plunkett 1973 and Tod 1832).

Recent history of the Dera estate boasted of the accomplishments of the Thakurain Dariao Kunwer, the widow of Raja Madho Pratap Singh. Recognized as a woman of extraordinary ability who not only held her own for 25 years but also added to her estates and possessions, she was succeeded by her husband's nephew Rustam Sah, who gave the British considerable assistance during the Mutiny and was rewarded with the title of raja (Bahadur 1978). Thus family histories of several taluqas reveal that in spite of seclusion and the institution of purdah, taluqdarins and ranis not only efficiently managed estates in the absence of male heirs, but also augmented their holdings by thrifty management and efficiency. Far from being perceived as aberrations, these facts suggest continuity with the mythical and historical traditions of *gaddee* families wherein the valour and heroism of Rajput women was legendary.

TALUQDAR RESPONSES TO THE SUCCESSION ACT OF 1869

The extent to which the existing institution differed from the colonial legislation has already been shown. While preserving the outward form of the traditional system, its content had been considerably transformed. Though this was a measure calculated to woo the taluqdar body, it was not uniformly hailed by all taluqdars. In fact it met with much less approval then the British expected, especially among Muslim taluqdars such as Saiyids and Sheikhs who were enjoined by tradition to give proprietary rights to collaterals in villages, according to Islamic tradition. Protesting against this measure, the taluqdars of Pirpur, the brother Syed Ghazzafer Husain and Syed Baqar Husain petitioned for equal proprietary rights to be assigned to all collaterals. They insisted that the same rights enjoyed by male relatives be given to adopted male members as well.[12]

Where the deceased taluqdar had no direct male relatives, succession to the estate posed a major problem and a will was necessary in such circumstances. Wills, unknown in Awadh until colonial times, began to be used to occasionally disinherit legitimate heirs. In the case of *Brijraj Koer* vs. *Mahadeo Baksh*, a will was used by a childless taluqdar to block succession by all collaterals he deemed totally unworthy, women whom he regarded as incompetent, and reversioners, who, for one reason or another, were considered wholly unsatisfactory (Oudh Cases, 1916: 33). In his will, the taluqdar expressed his misgivings about his reversioners, pointing to the dearth of relatives in whom sufficient confidence could be reposed as heirs. He identified two collaterals who would however have no more than a life-interest in the estate, a clause which led to considerable litigation subsequently.

Succession to the Samarpaha taluqa was a unique example of a situation. The estate actually passsed out of the hands of the childless taluqdar's own (Bais) clan, into the hands of the Amethiyas, the natal clan of the taluqdarin (Oudh Cases, 6 July 1917). When *sanads* were being granted, the taluqdar had already died without heirs and the taluqa was in the hands of the nineteen-year old taluqdarin. By the proclamation which declared that all those who were in possession at annexation would be confirmed in their holdings, the taluqdarin Dariao Kaur was conferred the *sanad* in 1861, which gave her full alienable proprietary rights.

Dariao Kaur died intestate in 1893. She had earlier executed a will declaring Sher Bahadur, a near collateral of her husband as her successor but revoked and cancelled it when Sher Bahadur claimed that the widow was wasting the property by giving it to her own relatives and that the property would pass away from the family to which it belonged. This in fact did happen as the taluqa on the death of Dariao Kaur passed on to Raja Rameshar Baksh Singh, a member of the Amethiya clan and grandson of the taluqdarin's brother. The court decided in favour of the latter on grounds that with the granting of the *sanad*, full proprietary, alienable rights had been conferred on the widow.

Interestingly, the court's argument against the collateral and in favour of Rameshar Baksh hinged on the interpretation of primogeniture by which the estate was to descend in the event of the grantee or any of her successors dying intestate. The courts ruled that the operation of the rule of primogeniture can be prevented by the exercise of the full power of alienation which has been conferred on the grantee (Oudh Cases, 6 July 1917: 33). This included full powers to alienate the estate, either in whole or part by sale, mortgage, gift, bequest or adoption to whomever the proprietor might please.

IMPLICATIONS FOR WOMEN

At any given time during the British period it was possible to find at least four or five female proprietors in each of the twelve Awadh districts, holding life estates in the absence of immediate male heirs. While by virtue of customary laws it may have been possible for portions of taluqas to be inherited by women, the compulsory adherence to primogeniture froze the relatively fluid situation regarding inheritance. Through the Act of 1869, widows of taluqdars had only a life-interest in the estates, and after their death, the property reverted to the nearest collateral male heir. While male taluqdars continued to enjoy the privilege of granting gifts of land during their lifetimes, taluqdarins appear to have been prevented from this. After 1869, court cases concerning gifts of land by deed, executed by widows show their being invalidated on grounds that widows had life-interest only.[13]

For all practical purposes, the widow acted as a trustee of the property during her lifetime. Attempts by taluqdarins to mortgage portions of their estates to raise money or to make gifts of land could be prevented by the ever-vigilant male reversionary heirs who treated such actions as an offence to their title in their estate. The courts invariably supported the male heirs in such cases.

Taluqdarins, often harassed by their deceased husband's male relatives, were even grudged life ownership. In an extreme case, an agnatic nephew was able to obtain ownership rights in one village which remained with his aunt, the ex-taluqdar's widow. Upon receiving the taluqa he immediately also claimed rent on her land, thus attempting to convert her into a mere tenant (Oudh Cases, 1921: 261).

An example of this tendency is provided by a case, *Hasan Raza Saiiyid* vs *Nawab Basti Begam*, where a Muslim widow was sought to be evicted from her house by the reversionary heirs, the taluqdar's nephews, on grounds that a Shia childless widow is not entitled to the immovable property left by her husband and that it should revert to the husband's heirs. The court argued that as the widow had obtained possession of the property on the death of her husband, peacefully, quietly and without fraud in lieu of her unsatisfied dower debt, the nephews were not entitled to oust her until the dower debt was satisfied. Since it was not proved that the amount of the widow's dower debt exceeded the value of the property, the court decreed that either Rs. 25,000 be paid to the widow or the house should remain as her property (Oudh Cases, 1912: 257).

Such patterns were replicated in the revenue-free villages in taluqas where grantees had died heirless, owing to which the holdings may have come under the proprietary possession of women. In such cases, women may have found themselves fending off enemies on two fronts, the claims of successors of the original grantors as well as the reversionary heirs of the husband. In *Wazir Mohammed* vs. *Har Pershad*, it was the taluqdar grantor's son and heir, who attempted to wrest a village from a woman on grounds that the original grantee having died sonless, the village was practically abandoned, not cultivated and in the incapable hands of the grantee's daughter. It was revealed that the grantee had in fact ensured, while still alive, that mutation of the village was made in his daughter Sardei's name. The grant deed allowed the grantee full heritable, though not transferable and alienable rights. The courts ruled that the deed was valid, that Sardei was indeed the heir and that the village would pass to her descendants. It was found that court proceedings had been initiated on the death of Sardei, emboldened by the lack of male heirs. Sardei's husband was found to be managing the village for their two daughters, the heirs (Oudh Cases, 1912).

As wives and mothers were considered heirs only in default of all male lineal descendants, adopted sons, or other agnatic heirs, such women as did get life ownership of taluqas, were keen to expand their estates during their lifetimes. There are several instances of taluqdarins attempting to make gifts to their natal family and to daughters, from thrifty management and surplus earnings. Baba Ramchandra's contention that taluqdarins were even more oppressive and exacting in their dealings with tenants may therefore be traced to a sense of urgency in amassing savings during a lifetime. Moreover, excessive reliance on the exacting tactics adopted by estate bureaucracy, the zilledars, sipahis and other estate functionaries contributed to the savings.[14]

The case of the twin taluqas of Sihipur and Khapradih illustrates how the Act worked against the interest of widows. The widow Thakurain Raghunath Koonwer received the *sanad* for the taluqa of Sihipur. In 1877, she executed a gift in favour of her brother's son Thakur Bisheshwar Baksh Singh who was a Bais Rajput. At this she was sued by her younger co-widow Thakurain Ramanand Koonwer and also a male collateral Ram Swarup Singh, the owner of the Khapradih taluqa. Eventually the deed of gift was cancelled by a decree of the Privy Council on the grounds that widows have only a life-interest. The legal heir was declared to be Ram Swarup Singh, the nearest collateral and also the taluqdar of Khapradih. In 1886, the taluqa of Sihipur was heavily indebted and in 1891, the widow Raghunath Koonwer died. In 1896 by a civil court decree, the taluqdar of Khapradih was declared proprietor of Sihipur as well. The property was thus amalgamated into a single taluqa,

Khapradih-Sihipur. Sihipur comprised 36 villages and 33 portions of villages and Khapradih had 197 villages and 117 portions.[15]

The Act of 1869 had therefore not only a built-in bias against women but the institution of primogeniture also threatened the very existence of smaller estates which were deprived of male heirs over a long period.

SOCIAL AND POLITICAL IMPACT ON TALUQDARI WOMEN

The Act deprived taluqdari women of some of the advantages they may have enjoyed under the personal and customary laws without compensating them in the economic sphere, as in the case of taluqdars. Its long-term effects on women were therefore debilitating, leading to an acceptance and reinforcement of existing patriarchies. The lowered status of taluqdari women leads to the questioning of assumptions about gender parity within a class. Despite belonging to a class which was the highest in the agrarian hierarchy, taluqdarins remained subordinated.

In the case of Muslims, the Shariah had ordained that daughters receive as inheritance, half the amount received by the sons of a deceased father. This advantage, along with the possibility of instituting *waqfs* (endowments), was now lost to Muslim taluqdari women and restricted their ability to inherit lands and estates according to Koranic injunctions. Muslim women who initiated a law suit had to contend with the handicaps created by customary restrictions on the movements of women of respectable families. Though some women did appear in court, many had to conduct their cases through male agents (Kozlowski 1989: 127). Instead of the empowering image contained in the folk accounts of ranis and taluqdarins where *gaddee* was well known, the political reality for taluqdarins was now characterized by an altogether unseemly dependence on estate managers. In a case narrated to me, the dowager maharani of the Ayodhya estate was known to cook her own meals daily for fear of being poisoned by the estate manager. On the Meopur-Dahla estate, the estate manager contrived to get his young niece married to the eighty-year old taluqdar in hopes of usurping the estate after their marriage.[16] On the other hand, there is evidence which points to successful and efficient management of estates during the life-tenures of taluqdarins of the Dera, Khapradih-Sihipur, Meopur-Dhaurwa and Kurwar estates.

Ill-equipped by training and experience in the management of finances and accounts, and limited to the confines of purdah, taluqdarins appear to have been exposed to manipulation and exploitation by unscrupulous estate managers. This vulnerability was inevitably utilized by the state to intervene in the internal affairs of such women-headed taluqas under the guise of the Courts of Wards. Where meeting the exorbitant revenue demands became the sole reason for the existence of estates, the powerlessness and political inadequacies of taluqdarins became the lever with which state control could be enforced.

It was the state's primary concern that revenue demands from taluqas would be met promptly and in full. This was in fact the purpose for which the settlement with taluqdars had been made. Hence, shortfalls in revenue were regularly attributed to inefficient management or to the extravagance and unnecessary expenditure indulged in by taluqdars. Administrators were alarmed to note for instance, that in 1864, at the wedding of the niece of Raja Rustam Sah of Dera, the wedding party consisting of 35,000 was fed for six days. Realizing that such expenditure would lead to chronic default in the state's share of revenue, long-term indebtedness and possibly the break-up of estates, the state intervened to dissuade taluqdars from undertaking such expenditures. As the government frowned upon the customary celebration of lavish weddings, the matter was taken up by the British India Association (BIA).

At the occasion of the Dera wedding, the chief commissioner wrote,

> It is astonishing that taluqdars should consider the fame and dignity of their houses promoted by a prodigality that must bring ruin on them. Another such celebration of marriage as has just taken place at Dera will be the ruin of that noble and loyal family, an event that would cause the government deep regret. . . . The example set by taluqdars is imitated by their humbler kurmies, small proprietors driven to mortgage and sell their properties to provide funds for a marriage, and it is truly said that a rajput will throw away an inheritance to celebrate a marriage.[17]

At the insistence of the government, the taluqdars' association (the British Indian Association) was encouraged by the government to adopt a resolution in 1864 that (1) no Kshatriya would borrow superfluous paraphrenalia such as camels, elephants, horses for a marriage ceremony; (2) that the bridegroom's father should take no more money from the bride's father than would simply suffice to entertain wedding guests; (3) that Kshatriyas would marry their daughters to none but men of equal rank; (4) that marriage expenses on festivities should not exceed half of the individual's annual income.[18]

Couched in the language of social reform, the resolutions attempted to alter the very logic of Rajput kinship and questioned the basis of alliances which informed Rajput polity. In the totality of social relations which were characterized by hierarchy and subordination even among ruling groups, hypergamy meshed easily with political power and status hierarchies. At a superficial level, wedding expenditures, including dowries, were indicators of a ruling family's status. As it has been shown in an earlier section, these were closely tied with the hypergamous marriage alliances, lower status brides being married to higher status grooms. In this context, while the lavish weddings afforded the opportunity for the bride's family to attempt to bridge the status disparity, they also served the more significant function of forging new political alliances and cementing old ones. Resolution three seemed to question the very roots of these age-old hypergamous arrangements. The resolutions struck at customs and traditions which, from the colonial perspective, appeared inconvenient for a progressive landholding group like the taluqdars.

At a political level, adherence to the state's suggestion that Kshatriyas marry their daughters only to men of equal rank would have achieved the wider objective of neutralizing the political strength of ruling clans. Traditionally, affinal and maternal relations buttressed the position of rajas vis-à-vis disgruntled collaterals. Such alliances could also act as a check on the potentially threatening rivalry between powerful clans. As marriage alliances were the traditional avenues for mobilizing political support for conquests and territorial control, in the altered political environment, these strictures would have ensured that ruling houses remained fragmented and politically weak. This reality from Awadh substantiates the rich anthropological and historical literature from a range of pre-colonial societies that have recognized the political purpose, functions and significance of appropriate matrimonial alliances among powerful ruling clans (Trautmann 1981). In befriending the taluqdars, the policy attempted to ensure that any threat to the colonial state emerging from the politico-martial alliances of taluqdars could be eliminated.

It is no wonder that taluqdars of Awadh were seldom able to abide by any of the BIA's resolutions, especially since, as already seen, they had affinal links in the North-West Provinces and Rajputana, where the BIA writ did not run. The Bais clan for instance would not give daughters to any Rajputs of Awadh as they were considered socially inferior to those of the west. For the Rajkumars and Bachgotis, it was an ambition to marry their daughters to the Gorakhpur Bissens and Surrats. Thus the co-operation of the chiefs of Rajputana, Mainpuri and Rewa was indispensable.[19]

The higher the status of the taluqdari clan, the more difficult was it for brides to find suitable grooms within the Awadh districts. Both custom and preference dictated that high-caste women moved farthest away from their natal villages. Thus in keeping with the north Indian post-marital residence norms observed by several scholars, higher-status brides were married into prestigious clans at increasingly greater distances away from their natal villages (Agarwal 1994: 140-6). If such post-marital residence patterns are seen in the light of the historical references to gifts of land made to brides by their natal ruling clans, significant questions arise about the nature of the control exercised by the brides themselves and the nature of access to the produce of the land. Evidence from Rajasthan relates to Rajput women Bhomias receiving proprietary rights in the village through dowry (cited in Bhadani 1980). It needs to be explored whether, in fact, high expenditures at weddings including the dowries given, were not in a way also a compensation for the uprootedness caused by post-marital residential arrangements accompanied by the brides' loss of meaningful rights in their natal taluqas.

CONCLUSION

The class of taluqdars had been in existence long befor the coming of the British but with colonial intervention, its complexion was altered and the term came to have different connotations from those in the past. As taluqdars were visualized by the state as revenue-paying intermediaries and mere landlords rather than rulers of men, the taluqdars' legitimacy was eroded both in their own eyes as well as in those of their collaterals and subjects. The colonial state worked on the assumption that the taluqdars' common economic background and status, their common goals of safeguarding their own interests and those of the British, and their distinct lifestyle would instil among them a consciousness of their class. In the long run, such a consciousness was expected to generate a sense of unity within the body which would be beneficial in safeguarding the interests of the state and also in achieving the support of the masses for British rule as a whole. By the turn of the century, the British were realizing that the result of their policy was not as intended; that assumptions about taluqdars as natural leaders were erroneous and misplaced. Deprived of traditional sources of power and legitimacy and isolated from the people they had once governed, the taluqdars were unable to play the role cut out for them. The legislation enacted to safeguard the estates from the effects of partition, played up the already existing cleavages between taluqdars and their kin groups.

Nor was the position of taluqdari women strengthened as a consequence of the economic privileges conferred on the male members of the class. Losing the flexibility of customs, women experienced greater restrictions and even discrimination vis-à-vis male members of their class. The strengthening of patriarchal control was manifested in a range of situations: the limited estate of widows; vulnerability at the hands of estate bureaucracy; the intervention of Courts of Wards in women-headed taluqas; subjection to protracted litigation at the behest of collaterals and women's unpreparedness in terms of education and skills to interact with officialdom, courts and the public domain. Stricter conformity with the patriarchal norms and traditions of purdah were enforced as the very logic of primogeniture dictated women's subordinated role as mere providers of heirs to the *gaddee*. Women's passive role as pawns in a complex system of hypergamous marriage arrangements was necessary to ensure that alliances of a political nature could be furthered, thereby strengthening the women's natal lineages. The threat to this well-articulated system which was posed by the BIA resolutions could not succeed owing to its roots in the ancient customary traditions as well as its geographical spread, beyond the confines of the Awadh province.

Despite belonging to the most privileged class in the agrarian structure, the subordination of these women continued. The archival sources and nature of the court cases over a fifty-year period, point to the contentious issues with regard to landownership which contributed to the increasing alienation of taluqdars from their kin. Customary traditions and practices among ruling Rajput clans of Awadh reflected a range of variations with primogeniture as it was introduced by the Act I of 1869. These variations also point to the flexibility of local customs and their resilience in the face of conflicts which threatened to tear apart the social fabric. The field of kinship studies and the sociological analysis of empirical evidence relating to descent, kin and affinal ties of ruling clans, offers possibilities for locating women within caste, clan and property structures.

My enquiry also foregrounds the centrality of historical perspectives in the analysis of kinship and gender relations. As women are located within networks of marriage, family and kinship, these areas become focal points for the analysis of impact of economic, legal and political processes on women. Assumptions about supportive roles played by kin and clan and family ties, may then be questioned with reference to women's experiences.

The next chapter will examine the long-term implications of another colonial legislation, The Land Alienation Act of 1894, for the inhabitants of a single village, Sarai Mohana. As seen in this chapter, though the Taluqdari Succession Act of 1869 was introduced to create a class of ruling elite, which would be loyal to the colonial state, its unstated consequences were detrimental to women of the very same class. The Land Alienation Act of 1894 which was intended to empower the state to procure land for public purposes, marginalized the peasantry, particularly its women. This study of Sarai Mohana is illustrative of the continuance of the anti-women development processes, which were set in motion by the Act.

NOTES

1. Secy. Ch. Commr., Lucknow, 24 April 1860, July 1880. Board of Revenue, Oudh Government. U.P. State Archives, Lucknow (hitherto UPSA).
2. MSS. Eur. F 116/100, India Office Library, London (hitherto IOL).
3. 'Form of Sanad'. Revenue A 25-8, Foreign Department Consultations, 1862. National Archives, New Delhi (hitherto NAI).
4. MSS Eur. F 78/95, p. 94, IOL.
5. Administration of Oudh, MSS Eur. F 78/95, IOL.
6. Ibid.
7. 'Partition of taluqa Maniarpur', Office of the Board of Revenue, 503 A, Dept. II, serial 1/26, 1915.
8. Oudh Government, 102, 1860-9, p. 97. UPSA.

9. V. 5992, IOL
10. Papers Relating to the Administration of Oudh, MSS Eur. F 78/95, p. 65, IOL.
11. Foreign Dept., General Branch, 28. Consultation 1864. On the Alleged Curtailment of Marriage Expenses Among Rajputs. National Archives, New Delhi.
12. Board of Revenue, Faizabad 478, 1860, UPSA,
13. Board of Revenue, Faizabad 423, UPSA.
14. File 10, Instalment, 1932, Nehru Memorial Museum & Library.
15. Board of Revenue, Faizabad, 423, 1893, UPSA.
16. Ibid.
17. BIA, 638, Lucknow, 28 Foreign Department General, Consultation, NAI.
18. On the Alleged Curtailment . . . , op. cit.
19. Ibid.

CHAPTER 4

Saga of the State, a Village and Landless Women

A public man is supposed to be working for people's good; a public woman is a prostitute, a commoner.

Joan Landes, 1988, *Women and the Public Sphere in the Age of the French Revolution*, Ithaca: Cornell University Press (3)

For the women in the Third World, the State and civil society are both complex terrains—fractured, oppressive, threatening, while at the same time providing spaces for struggle and negotiation. State embeddedness as well as state autonomy therefore embody complex gendered relations that work against women, as well as providing resources for negotiation and struggle.

S. Rai, 1996, 'Women and the State in the Third World: Some Issues for Debate', in S. Rai and G. Lievelsky (eds.), *Women and the State: International Perspectives*, London: Taylor and Francis

This chapter interrogates the role of the state in constituting and sustaining the structures of subordination arising from differentials in the ownership and control over land, with particular emphasis on the implications of these for women. While many studies have explored the historical linkages and correspondence between ruling classes, landownership and power in various socio-economic formations, few have attempted to place women at the centre of these equations to establish connections between women's powerlessness, their lack of control over land and productive resources and the relative impact on gender relations of the relevant features of different kinds of states. How states may advance or thwart women's access and control over land is examined in this chapter through the lens of power structures. As the nature of the state itself is not fixed, showing significant differences over time and space, its relationship to gender is also an evolving and dialectical one (Waylen 1998: 1-14). Hence, the ways in which gender relations are constructed will necessarily vary under different state forms and the manner in which states evolve over time through different stages.

The state as an institution upholds the interests of the ruling or propertied classes (Poulantzas 1978, 1979). Questions relating to the manner in which historically specific forms of states contribute towards institutionalizing gender practices, particularly those which have a bearing on women's access to land as a productive resource, remain relatively less examined. As states represent a variety of interests and are continually transforming, specific state policies and their implications for women's access to resources need analysis on a case by case basis. What follows is an attempt to compare the construction of gender relations within the Peshwa and the Mughal states, though these were apart in both time and space. Certain policies adopted by these states had a direct impact on the accessibility of land to certain classes/castes/categories of women. I examine the historical evidence from the Peshwa and Mughal states to probe the extent to which states in the past have reflected gender inequalities, how these have been heightened, and the overt as well as inadvertent ways in which states constitute such inequalities. My evidence, confined to northern India, is selected for its illustrative potential to highlight processes by which states in their compulsion to uphold the interests of ruling classes also uphold patriarchies and gender disparities.

A major section of the chapter is a case study, which analyses the impact of state policy on a single village, Sarai Mohana, over a fifty-year period since Independence. The historical insights from earlier sections are subjected to more intensive scrutiny at the micro-level, within a geographically-defined area and delimited time span. I first examine the state's approach to land and how it inadvertently refurbished existing inequalities not only between classes but also between genders. I then explore ways in which women's struggles are likely to impact on the state and are in turn impacted on by the state. This is also illustrative of the possibilities and strategies of action available to women in the context of a developmental state. In the light of the historical and contemporary evidence examined, the final section of this chapter arrives at certain conclusions about the limits and possibilities of the state.

Soon after Independence, the emergent post-colonial state in India was seen as potentially transformative, bringing about economic and social change with social justice being a prominent facet of its political rhetoric, a fact which has significant implications for women's property rights (Rai 1996: 33). Like other post-colonial states which, through their constitutions and legislations, sought to change and develop societies affected by the experience of colonial exploitation, the Indian state's progressive policies aimed at creating a just and equitable society with social benefits percolating down to all its segments. These aims were to be achieved through the interventionist role of the government. It is in this context that its potential to further and uphold the interests of women needs to be understood. The exercise assumes significance as sections of the women's movement have seen the state as the arena for both struggle and negotiation. As the post-colonial state evolved, its rhetoric of equality, including gender equity as enshrined in the Constitution, were gradually eroded in the course of implementation of policies. In a state characterized by a 'lack of political will', assertion of rights came to be seen as a significant means by which sections of the women's movement could pressurize the state. Since the 1980s, the demand for rights to land emerged as an integral part of the struggle.

Interrogating the state in the light of the impact on women of its liberalization policies, assumes greater urgency today. The first three decades of state intervention characterized by the three-pronged land reforms—abolition of zamindari or feudal landholdings, land ceilings and emphasis on redistribution of land and legislation to secure the rights of tenants—successfully achieved only the first of the aims. Far from completing the unfinished agenda of land reform, particularly land redistribution, a paradigm shift towards liberalization has resulted in significant implications for women and the state. As land reforms are not a priority and no wide-ranging agrarian transformation is under way, women are the worst hit, especially as most women are concentrated in the agrarian sector. Women's opportunities in agriculture are further shrinking and as they are excluded from the organized sector, low paid jobs go to them. Not only is there a decline in the employment of women but also in the conditions of work. The retreat of the state poses another dilemma for the women's movement in that, for decades, women have strongly criticized the state but must continuously turn to it for a guarantee of rights. Paradoxically, sections of the women's movement today are pressing for the restoration of state controls, while recognizing that the state represents the interests of the propertied classes. It has been argued that the state has a multiplicity of languages wherein the reluctance to upset the gender hierarchy takes precedence, hence the disjuncture between the state's official position and its practices.

The implications that state policies may have for gender relations, particularly women's access to and control over land is examined with reference to the Mughal and Peshwa states in the following sections. The historical evidence here is an attempt to enrich one's understanding of the ways in which states have dealt with the question of women's rights to land in the past and to provide clues about the possibilities inherent in states, including what may be expected on the issue from the modern Indian one.

STATE AND CLASS: THE MUGHAL STATE'S LAND GRANTS TO WOMEN

While the centrality of the state is not disputed, the nature of the state remains varied, with often an evolving dialectic and dynamic relationship to gender (Waylen 1998: 7). In different geographical locations and time spans, abundant evidence exists in support of the view that in general, states have historically supported subordination of women. As this hypothesis may need testing for historical evidence, two cases shall be examined. This evidence is also illustrative of the fact that the state itself is a product of particular historical and political forces.

> If the state is not a homogenous entity but a collection of institutions and contested power relations, it is far better to see it as a site of struggle, not lying outside of society and social processes, but having, on the one hand a degree of autonomy from these which varies under particular circumstances, and on the other, being permeated by them. (Waylen 1998: 7)

Hence, gender relations are partly affected by the ways in which states are constituted. As such the state reflects as well as helps create forms of gender relations and gender inequality; state practices construct and legitimize gender differences, giving rise to gendered identities. These are constructed through legal institutions, discourses and ideologies generated by the state. Here my focus will be to examine ways in which states act to construct gendered subjects.

An examination of land grants made to women by the Mughal state illustrates the class character of the medieval state, the limits and possibilities of landownership for its women subjects and the rationale for conceding the privilege of landownership to only a very select group of women. Beginning with the reign of Akbar until the death of Aurangzeb, the substantial evidence of grants to women raises questions about the logic, rationale, purpose and nature of the grants, their scale and magnitude as well as class background of the beneficiaries. The state appears to have performed a paternalistic role in ensuring that women of propertied classes would receive a steady source of income in the absence of male family members. The maintenance of such aristocratic families was important to sustain and reproduce the social base of the state; it was crucial to do so even when the families in question did not have a male heir to serve the state. To prevent such families from breaking away was crucial in order to retain the distinction between the nobility and commoners, which in turn was essential for the validity and legitimacy of the state. By confining this privilege to a miniscule class of women, the state upheld firmly-entrenched patriarchies. Given the paternalistic logic of the grants and their *raison d'être*, the state did not envisage autonomy for women grantees but merely ensured that its class base was refurbished.

Under the *madad-e-maash* tenure, land grants were made to women which in most cases conferred full, proprietary, heritable and transferable rights. The grants were made to women of respectable families who had no other means of livelihood. They were charitable in nature though not always tax-free. Widows and young children were eligible for the grants and if the candidates were also 'good', 'pious' and 'god-fearing', their eligibility for the grants appears to have been further enhanced (Bilgrami 1988). Grants to women, termed *Chak-ha-e-Musammati*, were distinct from those made to men, *Chak-ha-e-Muzakerati*. The latter were made for considerations of scholarship, religion or piety, or to members of the nobility who were unable to take up employment owing to their exalted status. Women grantees could also hold lands collectively, the shareholders being women under the tenure *Farman-e-Musammati*. Grants to women were begun in the reign of Akbar and continued in later periods (ibid.).

In the initial years, as women grantees were not required to present themselves in court for verification and confirmation of grants, the question whether or not the original grantees or their heirs were alive, needed to be looked into. Also required was confirmation that the heirs were as deserving of state support as the original grantees. The state further needed to ascertain that the heirs had no other means of livelihood and that they were in possession of the verification deed issued by the court. All these administrative requirements led to the evolution of systematic procedures to ensure that adequate follow-up action could be taken on such grants. In addition, procedures were also in place for action on new applications and to ensure and establish the authenticity of claims (ibid. 1988).

In the early period, as there was no requirement for women grantees to present themselves in court for verification, grants began to be purchased by zamindars, *muqqadams*, and *chaudharies*. The government conferred on the grantee the right to enjoy the revenue from the land and exempted the grantee from paying cesses, revenues and taxes to the state. However, the occupancy rights of the tenants were not to be disturbed, nor were the zamindari or revenue-collecting rights in the area to be affected by the grant. Both fertile and fallow lands were assigned, so that cultivation could be extended. Grants were of two kinds: (a) those given for benevolent purposes which bound the grantees to pray for the prosperity of the donor, and (b) those granted on condition of service which were made to officials in lieu of salary. Usually only half the grant was confirmed in the case of heirs (ibid.: 88).

On the death of the original women grantees, the lands were divided among the female heirs in different proportions depending on their relationship with the deceased. In one case, Mussammat Zainab, the holder of a grant, transferred her holding to her own daughter Abida, and obtained a royal *sanad* for her. The latter died issueless and her nephews occupied the land and later obtained a *sanad*. Legal advice was sought when the stepmother of Abida claimed the land. The court verdict stated that the land could not be taken away from those who had already obtained the *sanad* (ibid.). It appears that fairly stringent legal procedures were followed for identifying proximity of kin to deceased heirless grantees for purposes of succession, and further that a sanad, once conferred, could not be reversed.

The fact that women had the right to control and dispose of their properties in accordance with their will and discretion is illustrated by an unusual case wherein Aurangzeb conferred 550 *bighas madad-e-maash* on the two widows and young children of Nawab Rashid Khan. The older wife received 300 *bighas* and the younger, 250. During her lifetime, the older wife, by means of a bestowal deed, made over all her property to her only daughter in order to ensure that the sons of Rashid Khan would have no claims (ibid.). In 1680, Aurangzeb issued a farman stating that since the grant was an *ariyat* (article of loan), not property, its inheritance was to be governed by imperial orders and not the Shariat. The rules were:

(a) A married daughter having some property from her husband was debarred from sharing the inheritance with her brother. If the daughter was a widow without any means of livelihood, and there were other female heirs, the son was to maintain them from the income of the grant.
(b) If a daughter was the only child of the deceased but there were other agnatic heirs (*asbat*), she was to be recognized as the sole successor of the property.
(c) The widow of a childless grantee was entitled to enjoy the deceased husband's estate during her lifetime. At her death, the estate was to pass on to the husband's heirs. In the absence of the husband's relatives, the land would belong to the wife's relatives.
(d) In case the mother, grandmother or some female Koranic heir survived the grantee, then the Muslim law of inheritance was to be applied.

It is clear that the medieval state's concern was to ensure that women of aristocratic families did not face penury simply because there were no male family members who could act as protectors and guardians. To the extent that women of a certain class, belonging to elite families who were in the state discourse 'deprived' of male support, could be rendered extremely vulnerable, the state was forced to perceive its responsibility towards this select group of women. The state saw itself as providing for the narrowly-defined needs of such women, and the provisions made for their support reflect these concerns.

That only few were singled out for support suggests that the needs of this class of women who were already privileged, were seen as legitimate and the maintenance provided was to ensure that no family from the highest class would face the alarming prospect of a slide down the status hierarchy. Most noteworthy is the state's presumption that propping up the women economically could stall such a calamity. The state was reinforcing established patriarchies wherein the honour of a class, reposing in its women, could be restored by granting certain privileges and assistance from the state's coffers. Interestingly, the state saw no contradiction in making grants of land to women and in no way did a person's sex disqualify her from holding land as a productive resource, a viable means of livelihood, and an income-generating resource. Further, that women members of already privileged groups became recipients of greater advantages appears to have posed no contradictions. That the state's concerns did not extend to women of other classes in society, reinforces theories about states representing and reflecting the interests of the ruling classes.

STATE AND CASTE: THE PESHWA STATE

Just as states have historically reflected class interests, so also have they traditionally upheld the interests of the upper castes. The close connection between the caste system and the state's enforcement of it and the manner in which the former developed and diversified, owing to state power is well exemplified by the Peshwa state in eighteenth century Maharashtra. It created a landed aristocracy recruited from Chitpavan Brahmin families who came to dominate the rest of the community. The Peshwa state upheld Brahmanical patriarchy and privileged brahmanism while suppressing the lower castes. It succeeded in this by ensuring that its bureaucracy as well as the legal apparatus of the state preserved the caste hierarchy, the code of conduct between castes and also privileged *shastric* over customary law. The state upheld a strict code for Brahmins and prevented other castes from emulating their practices, particularly the taboo on widow remarriage, thus ensuring the ritual distance and the hierarchical relationships between castes. The state further enforced the rules of untouchability, suppressing demands for better treatment of untouchables.

By consolidating and further legitimizing brahmanical traditions, the Peshwai sought to impart greater rigidity to the caste system. For instance, when individuals deviated from the traditional religious code of conduct, the state reserved the right to both remove as well as restore the caste status of individuals. The state further enforced the codes of conduct between and within castes. Rather, the internal functioning of caste rules and maintenance of established hierarchies was a matter of great importance for the state (Chakravarty 1998: 14-17).

Clearly the regulated conduct code for women was the index for caste ranking within the caste hierarchy. On the one hand, castes which allowed widow remarriage slid lower in the hierarchy, on the other, the state's efforts at ensuring that castes did not enforce the ban, thwarted the claims for higher status. Thus under Brahmanical patriarchy, strict controls on the sexuality of women not only ensured the purity of the blood line (and, hence, claims to higher status) but also served to maintain the different norms of each caste. To ensure legitimate marriage, the requirement was pre-pubertal marriage for women, thus ensuring that sexuality was harnessed to ensure legitimate reproduction. As the sexuality of upper-caste women was closely monitored and highly valued, these women were also most carefully socialized into the *pativrata dharma* of wifely duties and fidelity, so that women themselves became complicit in the structures of gender and caste (ibid.: 29). The 'adulterous low-caste woman' was as much a construction of the state as the upper-caste woman.

Further, demographic compulsions were such that Brahmin widows were withdrawn from active social reproduction so that the ban on widow remarriage among Brahmins also made demographic sense. On the other hand, as Kunbi women gave a class of producers in the fields, widows were encouraged to observe a form of marriage called *pat*. Remarriage for widows of the labouring classes made greater economic sense.

In comparing certain elements of the Mughal and Peshwa states which have a bearing on the theme of this chapter, a hypothesis which receives confirmation is that states tend not only to reflect existing power relations within society while upholding the interests of the ruling classes, but also strive to reinforce and strengthen existing class relations and hierarchies. Given the historical predilection of states to support and refurbish existing class structures, the interesting question that arises is: why then do sections of deprived classes, including women, expect to receive support from the state? Given this background, to what extent are deprived sections justified in their expectations, and what form do these expectations take in different social formations? Do the paternalistic concerns of states and their commitment to ensuring justice override class compulsions? What kinds of spaces are available to states to manipulate social relations beyond maintaining the status quo? The answers to these questions depending on the type of state under scrutiny, will have implications for current perceptions of states as sites of struggle, and in addition indicate the limits and possibilities which different types of states represent.

The Peshwa and Mughal states represent two distinct types with reference to the possibilities for women's ownership and control over land. While both states upheld the existing social order, the inadvertent effects of the policies were diametrically opposed in the two cases. Although the *madad-e-maash* grants of the Mughal state gave a limited group of women rights over land as a productive resource, these women from the ruling class could theoretically enjoy full proprietary rights over land only under certain specific conditions. The state clearly did not make a gender distinction with regard to proprietorship rights, where doing so would have meant a substantial decline in the numerical strength of the ruling class itself. Clearly, the state's interests remained confined to, on the one hand, empowering the class which constituted its support base and, on the other, making sure that cultivation would continue and even get extended as a result of the support given to the grantees. Hence, a limited group of women emerged as beneficiaries of the state's policies and concerns, enjoying an independent source of income from land in the event of widowhood or absence of male family members. This 'benevolent paternalism'of the state has, however, to be seen as an unintended consequence and fallout of a broader policy of support for the class as a whole and not directed in any way at strengthening or empowering aristocratic women per se.

In contrast, the Peshwa state's concern with upholding Brahmanical patriarchy, far from offering economic security to women actually succeeded in creating debilitating conditions of acute dependence on male family members, particularly among the ruling classes, comprised predominantly of Brahmins and Kshatriyas. In strictly enforcing caste codes regarding pre-pubertal marriages and taboos against widow remarriage as outlined in the shastras, the state endorsed a system of strict controls on upper-caste women which in effect also impinged on their productive roles and rendered them incapable of participating in socially useful productive activity including decision-making. Ritually, the upper-caste non-producing woman was the opposite of the toiling woman of the labouring castes, as the state enforced lower-caste codes with the same strictness as upper caste ones. The Peshwa State thus ensured that the class of producers was reproduced, and the caste system based on the ideology of hierarchy and separation between castes was maintained through rigid adherence and observance of the codes and taboos by each caste in the system. Neither group of women had access to land.

THE COLONIAL STATE LAND ACQUISITION ACT 1894

I shall now examine the colonial state's benevolent and paternalistic concerns, reflected in a legislation entitled the Land Acquisition Act of 1891 (later modified as the Colonial State Land Acquisition Act of 1894) which enabled the state to acquire land for a range of public purposes. Like their predecessors, the colonial rulers were concerned with acquiring land for public works, but the scale of land acquisition for projects ranging from the construction of the railways and roads to educational institutions, appears to have been unprecedented. The Land Acquisition Act was a mechanism for acquiring land for state purposes and a means by which acquired land could be passed on to individuals for the implementation of schemes to benefit the public, such as schools and universities. Exploring a limited set of problems pertaining to the working of this Act in relation to a single village, I examine in historical perspective the unintended consequences of the Act on gender in the village community.

The urgency of such an enquiry is highlighted by the fact that the Act of 1894, with minor amendments, continues to be in operation more than a hundred years after its inception. Also, the relevance of this enquiry is underlined in the context of globalization, where more liberal laws are being sought to be introduced, that would make land acquisition even easier for the purposes which the state and market deem necessary. Thus the historical evidence at one's disposal is a unique opportunity to analyse the processes of social change and marginalization set in motion by the working of the Act on the women of the affected agrarian communities.

The history of village Sarai Mohana since the operation of the Act, highlights the gap between the state's benevolent stance in its development projects for the common good on the one hand and, on the other, the processes of marginalization which often ensue, wherein women, landless and the most disempowered, are further marginalized so that exploitation, impoverishment and the disintegration of communities becomes inevitable. Throughout history, as the Act amply demonstrates, the landless who depend on the village as a community find that they lack the right to be compensated for loss of livelihood. Parallels can be drawn with the transfer of lands today to the corporate sector and the impact of such processes on communities for whom common property resources may be the only source of life support. A distinction exists between the class which gets the benefits, and the class which pays the price of development, particularly the women within the class. I get to examine what happens to agrarian communities when land as a productive resource is no longer available.

Land Conflict in Sarai Mohana

Sarai Mohana is a village located on the eastern edge of the city of Varanasi on the banks of the Ganga, at its confluence with the river Varuna. The village covers an area of 229 acres and stretches approximately 2 km in length. The population comprising approximately 700 households, numbers 10,000, which represents a steep rise over the 250 households that were in existence when the conflict began in 1935. The Ganga surrounds the village on its southern tip and the lands of the Krishnamurti Foundation Trust on the other three sides. The southern side of the village is being steadily eroded by the changing course of the Ganga. Erosion of say 25 m of land is expected in the next fifty years, and is likely to exacerbate the already acute land hunger in the village (personal communication, Pradhan V.K. Sinha).

The story of Sarai Mohana is one of continuing conflict with the Trust over the manner in which it came to acquire the village lands prior to Independence, rendering landless the original inhabitants. Intense land hunger, impoverishment, and marginalization of the villagers have escalated in the past fifty years.

VILLAGE POPULATION BY CASTE AND OCCUPATION

Table 6 indicates the caste and occupational structure by household of the population of Sarai Mohana today.

In 1936, the village was under the combined zamindari of absentee landlords Murtaza Husain and Fatima Begam, who resided in Mustafabad, some distance from the village. Cultivators of the Mallah (a fishing and boating caste) caste who comprised more than 75 per cent of the village population, along with other village cultivators, paid a yearly rent to the zamindars for the privilege of cultivating their leased plots of land. Out of the 250 families, 35 enjoyed some form of cultivating rights over the 75 acres of village lands, which were under cultivation. Castes such as Khatik, Nai, Kalwar, Dom, Lohar and Bharbhuja pursued their caste occupations within the village economy. In 1936, most of the village cultivable lands were acquired by the state through the Land Acquisition Act and made over to the Krishnamurti Foundation founded by Annie Besant to set up educational institutions.[1]

In addition, 40 acres of land were purchased from each of the zamindars for the establishment of an agricultural school and farm.

TABLE 6: CASTE AND OCCUPATION OF SARAI MOHANA HOUSEHOLDS

Sl. No.	*Caste*	*Households*	*Occupation*
1.	Mallah	450	Weaving 90%
2.	Chamar	100	Weaving, wage labour in town, fishing, sale of fish, labour, boatmen
3.	Khatik	15	Vegetable/fruit vending, weaving
4.	Nai	4	Hairdressing, weaving
5.	Kalwar	4	Weaving, petty retailing
6.	Dom	3	Cremation, sale of firewood
7.	Lohar	1	Iron mongering, wage labour
8.	Bharbhuja	1	Grain parching

Significantly, excluding the *abadi* (village settlement), the entire land of the village, including the village commons, waşteland, cremation sites and fallow lands were acquired by the state under the Land Acquisition Act of 1894 and made over to the Foundation. An agricultural college and a dairy farm were established by the Foundation on the acquired lands, and a small hospital and primary school were opened for the benefit of villagers.

Table 7 shows details of landholdings in Sarai Mohana which were taken over by the Land Acquisition Act in the year 1936.

The Land Acquisition Act in Sarai Mohana

The Land Acquisition Act observed the following broad procedures, despite numerous amendments made during its hundred-year history. (1) The government represented by the collector was to be requested for the land, through a proposal to be then examined by the collector and a notification issued. (2) The probable land losers were identified, the land measured and the compensation calculated. (3) In spite of the land losers *not* accepting compensation, the notified land was acquired and transferred to the requiring body, provided the collector was satisfied. (4) In case of dissatisfaction with land measurement, the amount of compensation, or its apportionment between the interested parties, the courts could be approached for redressal. Clearly, the law provided little scope for land losers to contest and prevent their land from being acquired, as they were compelled to fall in line with the conclusions arrived at by the collector. The collector-centric paradigm was particularly suited to the interests of the colonial state.

The Act of 1894 was enacted as a measure for acquiring land for public purposes, yet the 'public purpose' was left vague and undefined, *making it one of the most misused civil laws in the country* (Asif 1999: 1565). While the colonial state was able to acquire land for mines, plantations, railways, etc., later amendments introduced in 1984, further streamlined the process of acquisition, particularly for the corporate sector. Also, to this day courts accept as 'public purpose', the state's requirements, which includes transfer of land to the private sector as in the case of the Krishnamurti Foundation. Usually more land than is required for a particular project is obtained and then sold for profits (Fernandes 1998: 2703). After

TABLE 7: LAND HOLDINGS IN SARAI MOHANA TAKEN OVER UNDER LAND ACQUISITION ACT IN 1936

Type of holding	*Name of* kashtkar	*Caste*	*Number of plots*	*Area in acres*
Seer land	Saiyid Mohammad Ali, Son of Mutaza	Muslim	3	0.10
Seer land	Must Sogna Begum	Muslim	-	0.20
Seer land	Must Kaniz Kubra	Muslim	-	0.27
Occupancy tenants	Shiva Saran	Koeri	3	0.22
Unknown	—	—	22	2.47
Fixed rate tenants	Lakshmi Narain and Shiv Shankar	Kalwar	6	3.26
Occupancy tenants	Murst Baijanti	Kayastha	1	0.21
Fixed Rate tenants	Ram Deo Balaran	Brahmin	5	1.38
Unknown	—	—	13	4.24
—	Ram Khilawan	Koeri	5	2.0
	Bhusi & Gopuli	Faqir	7	1.79
	Ayudhya	Kshatriya	8	3.10
Occupancy tenants	Shiva Murat	Kshatriya	7	3.13
	Ram Baran	Koeri	3	0.57
	Sahdeo, Mahadev Ram Balan	Koeri	3	1.17
	Jitu	Chamar	5	0.49
	Moligin		4	1.60
	Bhunu, Gopali, Munu, sons of Faquir	Chamar		

Occupancy tenants	Ram Harekh, Shiva Harekh	Chamar	3	0.33
	Must. Janki	Chamar	1	0.41
	Bhaggal	Kalwar	2	0.69
Non-occupancy tenants (of more than 12 years)	Ram Hurukh Shiv Hurukh	Chamar	1	0.30
	Sheo Charan	Chamar	1	1.41
	Ram Das, Bhagwan Das	Khatik	1	0.15
	Jawahir	Bhar	1	0.34
	Bacchan	Chamar	1	0.30
	Munni Lal, Chunni Lal	—	2	0.50
	Bacchu	Chamar	1	0.27
	Jitu	Chamar	1	0.08
	Bhaggal	Kalwar	1	0.03
	Shiva Murat	Kshatriya	1	0.06
	Sitaram	Kalwar	1	0.52
	Binodi Fakir	Chamar	1	0.22
	Ram Deo	Khatik	2	0.75
	Sitaram, Ram Lal	Kalwar	1	0.90
	Jhingurlal	Kayastha		
	Kishan Das	Kalwar	4	2.00
Statutory tenants	Swamijis	Budh	10	8.41
	Manager	Sanyasi (Manager)		
	Ramlal & Sitaram	Kayastha & Kalwar		
	Shivnandan Ram Palat	Mallah	1	0.91

TABLE 7 Contd.

Type of holding	Name of kashtkar	Caste	Number of plots	Area in acres
Occupancy	Ajudhia Bahadur	Kshatriya	1	0.50
	Shiva Murat	Kshatriya	1	0.90
	Balran	Chamar	1	0.29
	Ram Das & Bhagwan Das	Khatik	3	0.99
Statutory	Medha & Rama	—	12	4.52
	Jai Kali Bahadur	Khatik	2	0.87
	Mussamat Lalji, Baijanti	Kayastha	1	0.40
	Ram Dhan, Ramsharan	Koeri	1	0.05
	Ayudhya Bahadur	Kshatriya	1	0.06
	Shiv Murat	Kshatriya	1	0.10
	Lalji	Kayastha	1	0.20
	Sheo Charan,	Mallah	1	1.20
	Puran Jhunjan	—	1	0.35
	Must Sahora	—	1	1.00
	Sayed Mubod Ali, son of Murtaza	Muslim	1	0.67
Fixed rate tenants	Must Lodhi	—	6	1.94
Occupancy tenant	Must Sheo	Brahmin	2	0.77
Statutory tenant	Ram Lal	Kayastha	1	0.30
	Thakur Das, Ram Nandan	—	1	0.45

Occupancy garden	Hur Lal Bahadur	Khatik	2	1.36	
Occupancy garden	Moti & Hira	Chamar	3	1.43	
Statutory tenant	Munni	Bhar	1	0.22	
Statutory tenant	Musst Dulari	—	—	0.06	
	Makundi	Mallah	1	0.10	
Statutory tenants	Rawal	Khatik	25	9.08	
Abadi			2	0.35	
Parti Jadid			1	0.77	
Parti Kadim			8	4.08	
Banjar			1	3.12	
Sui Gangaji			1	37.47	
Nala			1	—	
Rasta			1	0.47	
Sri Ramji Maharaj					
Sri Swami Sacchidanand			4	0.56	
				0.35	Samadhi, *Gaddi* & Public Well
				0.25	
				0.70	

1984, in the wake of the new economic policies, the state was further empowered to acquire land for private industry, through new amendments. Hence, while the Act was designed to facilitate state acquisition of land for the colonial project, the post-colonial state arrogated to itself even greater powers.

The Land Acquisition Act in both its colonial and post-colonial avatars exemplifies empowerment of the state through statute. 'The function of the state being both to make law, as well as to enforce it, the expansive power to determine what constitutes a public purpose, the resources over which the state needs control, the costs which must needs be paid in this process, including human costs, are naturally within the statutorily legitimated power of the state' (Ramnathan 1995: 46). In its post-colonial phase, the Act exemplifies a process within which justice and democratic procedures are sacrificed in favour of expediency and manageability. Thus, the affected people entered the process at a point where the public purpose had already been determined, the beneficiaries identified, and the communities to be compensated had become the cost, and the compensation itself monetized (ibid.).

The law gave little scope to an affected party to challenge the acquisition process or to demand fair compensation or rehabilitation. Under Section 17 of the Act, objections to the acquisition of the stated land had to be submitted to the collector within a month after the first notification, after which the state's recommendations on the objections were to be treated as final. The clause, which required those challenging the acquisition to submit a written application within 30 days, presumed people's literacy as well as considerable awareness of the judicial process. Sarai Mohana offers an example of affected individuals intimidated by the judicial process withdrawing their objections from the courts and without memory of the pittance they received as compensation. Moreover, as there is no compensation required to be paid for land not having individual *pattas* or title deeds, it is presumed to be state property and as such, the entire village was collectively cheated of its *gaon samaj* or village common lands.

Clearly, the collector was extremely powerful and further post-independence amendments vested greater powers in the state bureaucracy. The Act defined as 'interested persons' those to whom compensation would be payable upon acquiring the property. 'There must be a direct or indirect interest either in the title to the property or in the quantum of compensation. In its reductionist portfolio, the law has narrowed down the categories of persons the state will have to keep in its vision when it displaces persons from the land or the situs of any other resource' (Ramanathan 1995: 43). The law thus tended to fragment the entire community into individual claimants capable of establishing legally acknowledged rights, which could then be acquired by the payment of compensation. The device of compensation worked towards the exclusion of persons and communities and effectively extinguished the right of the person over the land, rather than seeking to ensure a positive effect of the public purpose, on the person from whom the land was taken away. As the latter's role was never envisaged within a democratic process of participative decision-making, the character of the transaction effectively reduced the person to a cost (ibid.: 44). Hence, by reducing every right and interest to a claim, in monetizing compensation and making compensation the only option available to the affected persons, the law narrowed the space for dissent towards the purported public purpose and left no scope for conceiving issues of displacement or resettlement.

According to recent historical memory, the aggrieved parties left the matter of compensation to be settled through legal channels, yet, being illiterate, ill-informed, and most importantly, unable to pay the court fee and meet the summons, most of the cases were withdrawn over time. It appears that villagers had more or less reconciled themselves to the loss of lands as a source of cultivation and had begun looking for other sources of livelihood. The greater sense of loss experienced collectively by the villagers was over the village commons, wastelends, fallow and cremation grounds. The loss of these lands led to further hardship and marginalization of village women. These lands traditionally belong to the *gram sabhas* and enable village *panchayats* to undertake welfare and development schemes such as school and hospital construction, but successive *gram pradhans* in Sarai Mohana found their hands tied. The problem acquired acute dimensions with population growth, since state-sponsored development either deliberately bypassed the village or simply did not reach it.

Sources of the Present Conflict

As the Act made possible the alienation of village lands to the Foundation, the broad contours of the current conflict raise significant issues regarding village commons for women of the village community, as well as access and control over land as a productive resource and land for house sites. Immediate issues which agitate villagers are: the lack of basic civic amenities (sanitation, community hall), medical facilities, and a government school in the village, overcrowded housing, phenomena which are ultimately traced to the sheer unavailability of land where these could be constructed. Women's politicization has occurred over the past fifteen years, during which village women have visited the Tehsil office, the kutcherry and the governor's office, and have staged dharnas and demonstrations to demand the return of community lands. For this, women have cases registered against them, a fact that empowers the police personnel to enter their homes any time of day or night.

The urgency of continuing the fight for the return of common lands is seen as the bedrock of all community-based government programmes. Sarai Mohana women, representing the militant face of the struggle, have been repeatedly warned against incurring the wrath of the Foundation owing to the power it wields. As a consequence of being compelled to encroach on the Foundation fields for their daily ablutions in the absence of sanitation facilities, village women have had inevitable and innumerable confrontations with the police. On several occasions they have been rounded up from the fields by the state PAC personnel on behalf of the Foundation. Attempts to terrorize the women and thus break the back of the struggle have only escalated the violence. In these struggles, the collusion of the state and the private interests represented by the Foundation, has been brought home to the villagers in the starkest manner possible.

Such incidents indeed have many parallels in ongoing conflicts elsewhere in UP between agricultural labourers and landlords wherein the balance of power is moving towards a less unfavourable position for agricultural labourers. For instance, in a Jaunpur case cited by Jens Lerche, of conflicts between Thakur landlords and Chamar labourers, the confrontations typically involved a total physical and economic boycott of the Chamars by the Thakurs. The former were denied the right to cross the Thakurs' fields, to defecate in their fields or to collect fodder, and in addition suffered beatings when they dared to leave the Chamar hamlet (Lerche 1995: 495). Interestingly, during the course of my fieldwork, the very same restrictions placed on the Chamar community described by

Lerche were in operation against the Sarai Mohana residents, the landlord this time being the powerful Krishnamurti Foundation.

As the Sarai Mohana struggle is directed against the state and its beneficiary, the Krishnamurti Foundation, it gives us an opportunity to examine state policies that have consistently marginalized the landless and their women. In the fifty-year history of the village that this chapter is concerned with, there are three movements which have resulted in extreme powerlessness for women, and their separation from any kind of access to productive resources. First, land alienation resulted in lack of access to land as a productive resource and hence a pronounced shift to wage labour. For women were now unable to access or lease out even small plots for the cultivation of seasonal vegetables, which had once been a significant survival option for those of the fishing castes. As weaving of silk sarees became the mainstay of the village economy, the male-centred focus of this productive activity further marginalized women from technological knowledge involved in the process of weaving, leaving women with little option but to assist in the ancillary tasks of production or to seek unskilled labour opportunities in the city. Despite the crucial contributions of the women in weaving, their labour remains invisible, unrecognized and uncompensated, and thus perceived as peripheral. Clearly, here the adaptation to the weaving technology empowered male members, while women's labour was taken for granted, much along the lines of women of peasant households. Prohibition on fishing in the Ganga put a stop to fish vending, which had traditionally allowed women some control over income and resources, and a degree of autonomy and access to public spaces. Sarai Mohana became a supplier of wage labour, both male and female, to Varanasi city.

In contrast to the state-induced impoverishment seen in Sarai Mohana as a consequence of the lands passing over to the Krishnamurti Foundation, an elite girls' residential school has been functioning adjacent to the village since Independence. In addition, the Foundation ran an agricultural diploma college until 1985 and an agricultural training farm that is still flourishing on several acres adjoining the village. Ironically, Sarai Mohana villagers have been meeting their daily consumption needs through the produce raised on the farm for decades. Some villagers work for wages at the Foundation in various capacities. The greenery and prosperity seen on the Foundation lands presents a stark contrast to the rampant illiteracy, squalor, overcrowding, pollution and poverty of the village.

Until 1985, for almost four decades, despite continued dissatisfaction of the villagers at the loss of village lands to the Foundation, the rationale for reclaiming village lands remained weak and almost non-existent. In the mid-1980s, two developments escalated the present conflict over land and brought the issue of the restoration of the acquired lands to the Sarai Mohana *gram sabha* within the realm of possibility. A government order was issued, stating that all lands and buildings acquired by the Foundation were to revert to the government under the Zamindari Abolition Act [*Government Gazette*, U.P. Extraordinary, Vidhayi Parishisht, 15 October 1986, sd. Mohinder Singh, *sachiv*]. A subsequent government notification stated that from 15 October, all areas which were exempt from the operation of the Act were to be absorbed by the government of Uttar Pradesh, free of all encumbrances and liabilities (Document sd. Mohinder Singh, 15 October 1986; see Appendix I).

All lands that were formerly zamindari lands and had been acquired for educational purposes, had, until 1986, been exempt from the provisions of the Zamindari Abolition Act. Clearly, this was a significant loophole in the Act which had enabled landlords to save lands which would have otherwise come under the ceiling limits and thereby made available for redistribution under the scheme of 'land to the tiller'. It is therefore interesting to note that only as late as 1986 was an order passed to block this loophole. The implications of this late realization of the government were considerable for the natives of Sarai Mohana, since it raised expectations that once the acquired lands came to be vested in the state, the case for returning them to the village would be strengthened.

Another development of significance was the closing down of the agricultural diploma college as it was deemed to have outlived its purpose. The order signed by M. Srivastava, stated that the two-year-diploma colleges run by the Agriculture Department, being of temporary duration and recognition, were to be discontinued, along with other such courses in operation all over the state. A subsequent order relieved all teaching staff of their posts and hence the continuation of the agricultural farm attached to the Foundation was rendered both redundant and questionable. In spite of these orders, the Foundation continues to treat the agricultural training farm as its private enterprise, a fact that has become a bone of contention for villagers involved in the present conflict.

In 1988, after the orders were passed, the *pradhan* of the village filed a case stating that as the reason for which the lands had been acquired no longer remained valid, they should revert to the government. In 1988, a conflict arose over the continued occupancy of the lands by the Foundation, and fifteen villagers were arrested for disturbing the peace. Villagers' protests took forms such as participating in road jams, dharnas, hunger strikes, and demonstrations.

In 1991-2, ownership rights over 101 acres of land were awarded to the Sarai Mohana *gram sabha*, out of which 74 acres were found to be completely submerged by the Ganga all the year and obviously unfit for cultivation. The remainder of the land comprises a large ditch, some settlements and *banjar* barren lands. The need for the return of the communal land and wastelands had already been acutely felt by the villagers, hence the SDM's order allotting these 101 acres was seen as a positive step especially as this was also recorded in the *khasra* (field register) and *khatauni* (field records) of the village. However, the actual possession of the lands remained elusive, partly because a clause in the order stated that the lands would be returned to the *gaon samaj* once they were free of all encumbrances. During the course of the struggle, about thirty villagers forcibly occupied some lands adjacent to the settlement with a view to erecting homesteads. Until today, 140 acres of village lands are still occupied by the Foundation. The escalation of the conflict in the village can be traced to the moment when villagers demanded the construction of a primary school, *panchayat bhavan*, and women's centre on the *gram sabha* lands. The *pradhan* hoped that once possession was given, certain government schemes for villages would finally reach Sarai Mohana.

In its attempts to maintain control over the disputed lands, the Foundation adopted varying strategies such as building boundary walls and planting hundreds of saplings to justify retention of the lands. The villagers, especially women, systematically resisted these strategies. These acts of resistance pitted the women against the state's law-enforcing agencies and innumerable cases have been registered against different individuals for disrupting the peace.

These serial confrontations have escalated the scale of the conflict, as villagers are conscious of a heightened sense of injustice and see these as attempts to implicate them in false cases. For instance, the breaking down of the boundary wall caused cases to be registered against the villagers. The conflict was further heightened when village women collectively decided to resist the tree plantation drive by uprooting the saplings overnight. Although women argued that conversion of the field into a forest would jeopardize their safety and expose the village to criminal elements who could find shelter in the forest, one also knows that the transfer of land with trees on it would make the assertion of rights to it that much more difficult.

The Foundation officials resisted the state sanction of a hand-pump for the use of villagers in a congested part of the village, which would have serviced about 100-50 families, on the grounds that the lands belong to the Foundation. Consequently the government was forced to relocate the installation. Despite repeated demands from villagers for a free government-run primary school with the accompanying mid-day meal, life insurance, and free textbook schemes, the village remains without a school. On the other hand, the women actively resisted the sanctioning of a liquor shop and managed to have the site for the shop shifted. In resisting the liqour store, Sarai Mohana women were increasingly politicized and experienced a significant victory.

Not all village inhabitants have rallied around these common causes. A small though vocal section of the village community, which is linked with the Foundation, strikes a dissident note owing to its cooption by the Foundation. The latter has made a concerted effort to win over members of the community by offering them jobs in the Foundation. Not all individuals employed by it are able to resist, and hence represent a non-aligned apolitical front. To influence the villagers, tactics adopted by the Foundation have included lobbying; holding tournaments for youngsters and the award of prizes to winners; offering seasonal employment in agriculture to village Dalits on Foundation fields. The latter being numerically a minority vis-à-vis the Mallahs, the move tends to drive a wedge between villagers. Not all Mallahs are united in their opposition to the Foundation. Rather, a faction led by an aged Mallah teacher is vehemently opposed to the confrontational politics played by the majority of the villagers led by the *pradhan*.

Impact of Loss of Village Lands on Women

Lal Mani's is a typical Mallah household in Sarai Mohana. Lal Mani, who appears to be about thirty-two, lives with her three daughters, two sons, a mother-in-law and husband. The eldest daughter who seems no older than twelve is already married though she had not been sent to her husband's village. This daughter cares for the younger siblings and assists her mother in the household chores. The help provided by Lal Mani's eldest daughter allows the mother to spend approximately six hours a day reeling bobbins. None of the children has ever been to school, largely because the school run by the Foundation is unaffordable and government schools are non-existent. In order to supplement the family income occasionally, Lal Mani accepts work from *halwais* in Varanasi to roll out puris at weddings. For day-long services of this nature four or five times a month, Lal Mani earns Rs. 25 as daily wages. Perhaps the only member of the family who still maintains some connection with the former caste occupation is Lal Mani's mother-in-law. At six each day, the latter reaches the fish market and purchases a headload of fish for sale in the city. Having hawked the fish in Varanasi *mohallas*, sometimes without any nourishment, the mother-in-law returns home by around four with daily earnings of about Rs. 30.

The long-term consequences of the Land Acquisition Act have been particularly detrimental for women and eroded the security net which land had hitherto provided for women of the fishing and boating communities. First, at a single stroke in 1936, subsistence cultivation became impossible—all cultivable land was obtained by the Foundation. The non-availability of small plots for vegetable cultivation closed a significant survival option for women. This sudden closure of access to land or at least to labour opportunities on agricultural land within the village meant that women were forced to investigate alternative strategies outside the village on which the survival of families could be pegged. As pointed out earlier, fishing and river transport were also in decline, so that Sarai Mohana became a source of supply for wage labour to Varanasi city. The agrarian complexion of the village changed rapidly. Population growth over the years within the confines of the strictly demarcated habitation area, meant that in fifty years the village had been transformed into a teeming slum no different from the squatter settlements on the outskirts of major cities. Inhuman living conditions, and overcrowding in huts with inadequate sanitation and water supply, characterize the village today.

Loss of land was accompanied by a loss of community. In the meantime, however, a shift began to occur in the village's occupational structure, which to an extent contained the extremely disruptive trends that had been set in motion by the workings of the Land Acquisition Act. While adaptation to the changes in occupation appears to have saved the village from disintegration, it threw up its own set of challenges, particularly for village women. The occupational shift towards the weaving of silk sarees, being male-centred and mirroring classic home-based production, further marginalized the women. The male head of the household does weaving while the women, assisted occasionally by the children, carry out all ancillary jobs associated with production. In the process of weaving, the loom parallels the kisans' plough in the sense that the actual weaving cannot be done by women, the restrictions being both of a physical and ritual nature. A major task accomplished by the women every day in order to facilitate the process of weaving is the winding of the different coloured silk skeins onto the *charkhis*, i.e. the process of reeling. The silk is provided by the *grihasthas* in long rolled-up bunches which have to be wound tightly onto the *charkhis*. A reeling apparatus worked by the women makes it possible to wind the thread tightly on the bobbin. In addition to all their household duties, the women of the household spend approximately six hours a day on this task. Additionally, women arrange the vertical threads on the loom. In case of thread breakages, women may be called upon to readjust the loom. Women also take charge of the washing, curing and drying of the yarn.

Deepak Mehta's account of Muslim Julahas in Barabanki district, identifies four stages in the weaving process: yarn curing or sizing, reeling bobbins, warping and preparing weft members, of which the first two stages are supervised and controlled by the women of the Julaha hearth. Further, the generational division of labour ensures that while the son's wife coordinates sizing, the woman head of the hearth directs reeling in the ideal typical 'formed' household consisting of three generations (Mehta 1997: 38). Women reel bobbins in the zenana and not in the *mardana* or work shed which houses the loom and the warp beam (ibid.: 39). In Sarai Mohana, the spatial division into male and female zones was maintained, though without perhaps the same ritual significance attached to every stage of the weaving process as observed among Muslim Julahas.

The process of reeling has its own apparatus and implements, described in detail by Mehta (1997: 84). In the process of reeling, the woman's expertise is required to mount the yarn, operate the reeling apparatus, and ensure that the threads do not snap, especially when the yarn is being placed on the spindle. While the yarn is being rewound, it is twisted between the thumb and forefinger, so that it acquires tensile strength. After a sufficient number of bobbins are reeled, they are taken to the work shed. Further, Mehta points out that men ritually restricted from doing women's work, while women are prohibited from fashioning the weft. In a two-generation household however, the woman head often does the warping, but only because this type of household 'is in the process of negotiating its status as an independent hearth' (ibid.: 130).

The *grihasthas*, the middlemen who supply the yarn, make their arrangements with the male heads of households, yet there is an unstated assumption that women will invariably assist in all the tasks that constitute women's work in the weaving process. These assumptions parallel those of the hidden yet uncompensated labour of women of peasant households.

In a significant way, the shift to weaving represents loss of autonomy for the village women. In fishing, one of the traditional occupations in the village, Mallah women had customarily helped in the marketing of produce. This had provided them access to the marketplace and a degree of control over their earnings. Consequently, they were consulted in social, economic and religious spheres (Singh 1994: 898). In financial arrangements with *grihasthas*, on the other hand, women experience powerlessness and lack of control over the products of their own and their family's labour. In this sense, the new sphere of production makes use of pre-existing gender inequalities and societal assumptions relating to gender hierarchy 'to place women in subordinate positions at each different level of interaction between class and gender' (Sharma 1985: 57-88).

Tied to the process of weaving and other subsistence activities involving women, is the question of access to resources. Weaving represents a new technology, which was cornered by the men of the village, partly because weaving has always been male-centred.

The loom is set in a pit and involves continuous use of the legs as well as arms and considerable physical exertion.

As pointed out earlier, only 25 per cent of the 600 looms in the village are privately owned, the rest are rented out to the villagers by the *grihasthas* who supply the yarn, the pattern, the silk, and the *zari* threads. They also give loans and collect the finished product at a stipulated time. Consequently, production is carried out within the household with the weaver and his family having no say in the price of the product or in its marketing. As saree patterns are also supplied by the *grihastha*, the weaver exercises no autonomy in the creation of the saree either. Hence, the weaving household merely provides labour and skill, while the technology, raw materials, design and product belong to the middlemen. For a saree sold in the marketplace for Rs. 5,000, which takes the weaving household about thirty days to complete, the weaver is unlikely to receive more than Rs. 1,200. When a weaver needs a loan for the celebration of a marriage, the middleman would advance Rs. 750 out of a potential of Rs. 1,000. In this manner many weaving households are tied to the *grihastha*.

The meagre opportunities available to women for production are mat and bindi-making, involving low levels of skill and accordingly, low returns. The middlemen supply the raw materials required for production, but bindi and mat-making involve only the women of the household. As this productive activity is solely women's work and seen as a supplement to household income, it constitutes secondary activity with varying implications for the availability of women's labour and skills for household income, access to resources, credit, economic security, autonomy, etc. Women and girls earn on an average Rs. 6 for a day's work of approximately 12 hours making mats and producing the flaps of sticker-bindis. In bindi-making Rs. 2 is earned for 144 flaps! To supplement family incomes, particularly during the marriage season, women of all castes in the village offer their labour in Varanasi city to assist caterers at wedding banquets, rolling out chapatis. The seasonal and woman-centred nature of this work, deriving from women's home-making abilities, contributes to its supplementary character and low wages.

Displacement from traditional sources of livelihood has resulted in pushing women into the labour market at daily wages far lower than those paid to men. Gender-based differentials for agricultural work exist in the region, despite legislations. Often women shoulder alone the burden of supporting their family, even if they are not the sole earners. Lack of skills and training undermines their bargaining position in the household and outside. As women's labour is totally appropriated by the household, which regulates their work in the public space, access to any specialized or wage work could be denied or allowed depending on household needs. The extent to which women's employment is distress driven and hence exploitative, thus, requires assessment on a case-by-case basis.

Combined with the lack of schools and other training programmes, village women find themselves dependent and without opportunities for educational advancement, leading to a situation where most village girls and women are illiterate. This reinforces the relations of dependence, thereby perpetuating the structures of subordination wherein women accept piece-rate work at very low rates fixed by middlemen.The evidence from Sarai Mohana endorses Mies' findings that as women are being squeezed out of agriculture and not employed elsewhere, they are becoming pauperized at a faster pace than men (Mies 1980: 8-9).

CONCLUSION

Many occupational shifts undertaken by castes and subcastes are of more recent origin, connected to processes of modernization, changes in technology, skewed development priorities and programmes and, more recently, to factors such as globalization. The ensuing dislocations are economic and social in nature, involving several communities. While traditional sources of occupation disappeared, adequate alternative avenues were not forthcoming. Depending on their locations within the processes of production, the impact of these processes on the men and women of various communities was necessarily differential, though the predominant motif appears to be that of marginalization and pauperization, combined with the increasing polarization of the classes. Yet women end up being the most marginalized owing to the socially constructed disadvantages they face relative to men. The evidence from Sarai Mohana highlights some of the coping mechanisms and survival strategies adopted.

A gendered analysis of the impact of these processes in Sarai Mohana reveals that men and women are differentiated in terms of perceptions and expectations; nature of impact and access to new opportunities; resources and training; extent of political mobilization; capacity for organized and sustained political action; adoption of coping strategies; possibility for mobility, etc. As most of the work available for women is of an unskilled nature, with few possibilities of upgrading or refining traditional skills, the shift constitutes a move from subsistence-level existence to utter destitution combined with political disempowerment and cultural alienation. The deteriorating social and economic conditions are most in evidence among such fisher communities all along the Ganga, which are experiencing the loss of skills preserved and developed over centuries.

Therefore, if one moves from a description of the work that women do, towards an analysis of the ideological construction of tasks in terms of notions of appropriate work roles for women, one finds that women are landless, marginalized in weaving yet carrying out ancillary tasks as well as home-based work on bindi production to puri rolling, etc.

Nirmala Banerjee's theory of Indian women workers as a flexible resource at the disposal of the patriarchal family, illustrates well the nature of women's work in Sarai Mohana.

> To a large extent, the Indian household patriarch considers women of the household mainly as a flexible resource at his disposal: he utilizes it for any of an infinite number of functions including some of those in the public arena. But he retains the power to keep them vulnerable in the latter by controlling their basic access to productive resources, mobility and choices. This is done by ensuring that the ideology of the family orientation of women is not disturbed in any way. (Banerjee 1999: 331)

What is even more significant, she argues, is that the Indian state or other institutions have as yet not begun to interfere with this authority in any serious way for some specific reasons (ibid.: 332). For instance, the state has seldom attempted to bypass the household authority's right, which is always male, to decide whether or not women can avail of the technical and educational opportunities it offers. Historically the state has been oblivious to women as a category, differentiated or otherwise. Therefore the question of women's concerns as embodied in state policies has hitherto not arisen. It is only in recent years that the state has been forced to acknowledge the interests and concerns of certain limited sections of women, thereby opening up spaces and possibilities for struggles of different categories of women.

Read against the grain, the struggles of these women throw up interesting questions of women's resistance, powerful enough to make a real difference to the daily lives of poor women. The struggles themselves throw light on the processes of exploitation and domination and illustrate women's need for autonomy. The case has been highlighted since it allows reflection on landless women's interests, their agency and invisibility within democratic processes. Such collective struggles generate ways to think about mobilization and organization both as landless and as marginalized wage labourers. In the context of globalization, in the absence of land reforms and new technologies being appropriated by males, how are gender categories utilized in defining women's work? This case may thus be read as an illustration of a global process which draws upon indigenous hierarchy, ideology, and forms of exploitation.

NOTE

1. In 1895 when Annie Besant founded the Theosophical Society in the heart of Varanasi, its first branch had already been opened in Chennai. A society school and college were set up in the city, to be followed by a Trust for the social and economic development of rural society, for which land was required. Of the jungle land extending from the Varuna Sangam up to the Varanasi bridge, 97 acres in the possession of the Railway Department, was acquired and the Rishi Valley Trust was founded. A Montessori school and a hostel were constructed. The Theosophical Society school then shifted from the city to the newly acquired lands at the Varuna Sangam, and the complex, known hitherto as the Foundation for New Education, was renamed the Krishnamurti Foundation.

CHAPTER 5

Women's Marginalization: Tales from Bundelkhand

Jihi par vipata parat hai,
So awat yeh desh
Chitrakoot mein rum rahe
Rahiman Awadh Naresh

Only those on whom misfortune falls,
come to this land
The poet Rahim says, Ram the King of Awadh
also roamed the area around Chitrakoot
(when he was struck with misfortune).

R.H. Mitra, 1969, *Bundelkhand ki Sanskriti aur Sahitya,* Delhi: Rajkamal Prakashan (125)

No children were born of Janaka's lineage.
Sita was found lying under a ploughshare.
Sita goes off to live in the forest; thread is thrown in the chariot.
Sita goes off to live in the forest; she, the image of hard labour.
Sita goes off to live in the forest; a chariot and bundle of rags.
Sita, Rama's beloved, is going to live in the forest.
Sita goes off to live in the forest; there's a fig-tree in her path.
Sita has no one's support in her exile.

Songs of the mill-stone, comparing the plight of all women to the hardships endured by Sita. Sung by poor peasant women of Stri Shakti Mandal, Pune, cited in G. Poitevin and H. Rairkar, 1963, *Indian Peasant Women Speak Up*, Bombay: Orient Longman (60-6)

The struggle for ownership and control over land and other productive resources has emerged as a powerful instrument for women's empowerment since the 1970s. The articulation of this position within the women's movement has opened up a new area of debate in public policy. In the 1970s, the women's movement was reacting to the unfinished business, the promise of land reform, and also to the need to counter the premises of post-Independence development paradigms, such as gender congruence of interests within families, notions of unitary male-headedness of households, and of women solely as dependents. A sharp articulation of women's rights to land emerged from the peasant women themselves during the redistributive programmes of Operation Barga. It is thus possible to trace a historical link between the women's movement and the discourse on land reform. In this chapter I seek to explore the continued link between the two discourses. Underlying the analysis is the question to what extent is agrarian reform still central to any development strategy which seeks to benefit the least advantaged in society, including women.

The micro-level analysis in this chapter of land redistribution programmes aimed at benefiting the most marginalized communities in the Banda area of Bundelkhand, is an effort to bring visibility to problems connected with women's struggles for land and survival. The evidence is presented with a view to push forward the debate on women's rights to an exploration of the modalities and shape these rights are likely to take, particularly when the focus shifts from concerns of land inheritance for women of propertied groups, to control over resources and the products of their labour by the landless. This acquires significance in the light of the observation that 'the question of women's economic rights need to be understood within and as part of an overall strategy for economic transformation and development itself' (Agnihotri 1996: 528).

The structure of power in agrarian societies reflects the lack of distribution of land. It is hence no surprise that any meaningful land reform should aim at transformational change and succeed in altering the property structure and relations of production with a view to redistributing power and privilege. It must also address inequalities in access to other means of production besides land, as well as distribution and exchange. Implicit in this approach is that land reform means a reorganization of rights, privileges, and obligations in a system of production and distribution relations and is not necessarily or merely a rearrangement of physical plots (Herring 1983: 11). A rich body of literature exists on different variants of land reform in different regions, and the contradictory imperatives confronting the state, and in addition the lack of political will which ensures that land reforms remain incomplete.

There is however a crucial gender dimension that is missing from these analyses. As land reform itself has remained confined within male-centred development paradigms, this approach has further contributed to the incomplete nature of the land reform exercise. I shall now argue for gendered analysis of the impact of land reforms as well as for the need to focus on women as significant beneficiaries. It is the contention of this chapter that in agrarian societies, unless women of landless groups are included as a significant focus of redistribution efforts, the unequal power relations between genders will continue to persist. By implication, this position also constitutes a shift from an emphasis on property rights for women of propertied classes (in the sense of legal entitlement to land or inheritance rights) to strategizing for access and control over land for landless and marginalized women.

Two significant assumptions have contributed to gender insensitivity in the analyses of land reform, the slogan 'land to the tiller', where the tiller is seen as predominantly male, and notions of gender congruence of interests and equitable sharing of resources within households, which precluded *pattas* or title deeds being issued in the names of peasant women when land was redistributed. Among the premises and perspectives of the post-Independence development paradigms, the notion prevailed that sharing of resources would be equitable, and gender bias remained unrecognized. Second, the notion of the unitary male-headed household was even more deep-rooted, and harks back to colonial historiography which constructed the peasant as male, a feature which was uncritically accepted by Nationalist historiography and echoed in the post-Independence agrarian reforms. It is in the matter of land redistribution that significant breakthroughs are possible in redressing the imbalances caused by the above assumptions. Through concrete examples from the field, this chapter explores the manner in which these assumptions have worked against the interests of women. The effort here is also to examine how development processes often accentuate the already prevalent gender inequalities, in this case land reforms.

By the 1980s it was becoming increasingly possible to extend the reform rhetoric (redistribution to actual cultivators) to cover the category of women, especially as women's roles in agrarian production were systematically highlighted. However, while the demand for title to land carries forward the plank of redistributive justice, it tends to fall short of fully exploring avenues for strengthening women's access to resources and their control over them. Uncertainty and lack of clarity about the precise connection between women and land, is reflected in the manner in which the issue has been addressed by the women's movement.

There is also a need to reassess the prevailing belief within a section of the administration, that the goals of land reform have already been achieved, and that land laws now act as fetters on development processes, industrialization and capital accumulation. Moves by the state to review laws which have supposedly exhausted their utility, including land reforms, despite their inclusion in the Ninth Schedule of the Indian Constitution, have caused concern. For instance many tenancy and land laws by virtue of such inclusion cannot be challenged for violating fundamental rights. Hence while inclusion in the Ninth Schedule protects such laws from entrenched class interests, they are also protected from being challenged on grounds of gender discrimination (Agarwal 1995: A-39). Efforts to alter these laws so that the flow of funds can be directed to land and forest-related industries in rural areas; the relaxation of ceiling limits; the end of tenancy legislation; all these highlight the importance of micro-level enquiries.

It has been argued that land reforms have become a non-issue because of the state's inability to evolve institutions equipped to care for the concerns of the people. Access to land has become crucial to the struggle of the people but not central to official reform (Reddy 1991: 171). A commonly held view today is that land reforms have reached a point where they can neither increase production nor employment, so that reforms today are a non issue (ibid.: 180). On the other hand, the continued struggles all over the country for land mean that existing reforms cannot take into consideration the diversity of land problems in the countryside, which in turn cannot be solved without involving the people through their own organizations.

Reddy offers an administrative alternative to the top-down legislative role of the state in identifying decentralized village-level peasant and agricultural labourers' organizations playing a central role not only in identifying, acquiring, and distributing land, but also emerging as the basic organization for the provision of credit, other inputs, and infrastructural facilities. Grass-roots women's organizations could also play a meaningful role in this regard.

FOCUS OF ENQUIRY: MARGINALIZED WOMEN

A commitment to participatory democracy must necessarily involve a protection of the rights to livelihood and the right to life itself of the landless victims of development. If democracy is defined as 'the process by which individuals exercise control upon decisions which are regarded as collectively binding upon a community' then these individuals must also thereby be able to exercise control over the conditions which affect their lives (Chandhoke 1994: 2697). Hence, a just development policy would have to be one which has provision for women's access to productive resources and for their management of property (Thukral 1996: 1500). Findings of the development studies relating to displacement and rehabilitation have underscored this. For example in the policies governing the Tehri dam oustees, even when the woman is a '*khata* holder'(the holder of the title) and is entitled to a plot of land together with her husband, compensation has gone to the husband. Thukral concludes that in the absence of any affirmative clauses including women, who seldom possess ownership rights, they are automatically left out (ibid.: 1501). On the other hand, the experience of peasant struggles in other areas has been that 'by raising the question of land rights of women, rather than the peasant movement being divided, what is observed is its strengthening', consequent upon the greater democratization within the peasant movement as it attacks feudal landlordism (Nathan 1988: 549). Taking this idea to its logical conclusion, Nathan concludes that 'equal property rights for women, including the right to land, are essential for women to become full participants in the movement in their own right, and to prevent the strengthening of patriarchy that would inevitably follow a successful distribution of land solely to men' (ibid.).

The ramifications of access and control over productive resources are explored with respect to those classes of women who are also direct agricultural producers: poor peasants, agricultural labourers, and the landless. I situate this study within the most marginalized in rural Banda, largely because women of these categories are dependent on some form of agricultural activity for their own survival as well as that of their families. The labour of these women, whether on the field or in gathering forest produce, or subsistence-level cultivation, is essential for survival. As members on the lowest rungs of the agrarian hierarchy, these women are also the most marginalized by virtue of being women. The lowest rungs of Banda's agrarian hierarchy—the landless agricultural labourers comprising Kol tribals and the Scheduled Caste Chamars—were the supposed beneficiaries of the state's land redistribution programmes. What these schemes in their aims and implementation implied for women of these communities, is analysed here.

I focus particularly on the women of the class of agricultural labourers, those who are free to sell their labour, and those who are unfree or bonded and on women marginal holders who also take up seasonal wage work. In UP 80 per cent of the population live in 1.12 lakh villages, 85 per cent of livelihoods are derived from agriculture, 83 per cent are kisans and 21.40 per cent are landless. Women are solely dependent on agriculture and their contributions to agricultural production are more if not at least on par with those of the men of their households. Except for ploughing, these women do all kinds of hard work round the clock, yet their efforts remain invisible. To a large extent the overlap of caste and class hierarchies at the lowest rungs is marked, which makes for cumulative inequalities. Finally, in the moves towards globalization, it is these categories which face imminent marginalization.

The parameters of the current discourse on women's land rights has eclipsed the fact that not merely individual women but entire families and rural communities are dependent for survival on the ways in which women are able to access resources. As a corollary, the matter of strengthening women's bargaining position over a piece of land, 'a field of one's own' has emerged as the logical next step in posing the issue as one of women's property rights. Concessions from the state and activation of its legal arm to enact suitable legislation then emerge as the means of effecting social change.

It is partly in an effort to re-examine the terms of this discourse that I shift focus to marginalized, poor peasant and landless women. Moreover, the enquiry is prompted by the need to evolve strategies for rural women to promote greater access, autonomy and control over their own lives within specific socio-economic contexts and as active productive members of the distinct castes, classes and communities within which they are embedded. In shifting the focus from concerns of land inheritance from women of propertied groups to control over productive resources by those of landless and marginal classes, creative solutions for empowerment may be thrown up.

It may also be pointed out that the various legal enactments that affect women's rights to own land, pertain only to privately held land and not to state policy affecting the physical access to and distribution of public land (Menon 1996). The meaning attached to land takes on varied hues for different castes and sections of landless, small peasants and agricultural labourers. Where traditionally women have been denied independent rights to manage and control land, their access to and control over productive resources takes on added significance as it creates a space 'wherein a renegotiation of gender roles can occur such that women's independent right to land is acknowledged by the community as a socially legitimate one' (ibid.: 1). The evidence from the field highlights the fact that while women may have considerable rights to own and inherit land in the Constitution, the recognition and legitimacy accorded to these rights at the societal level may often be missing.

THE SETTING

Fieldwork was conducted in five villages, Rukmakhurd, Karonha, Hela, Kui and Gauriya, of Manikpur block in Banda district. Some of the villages border the forests of the Ranipur Game Sanctuary while at the southern tip, approximately 12 km. away from Rukmakhurd, lies the border of Madhya Pradesh. Described as an infertile area with inadequate water,

> This remote area contains all the horrors of rural India: bonded labour, seizure of land belonging to the tribal Kols by rich landlord classes, the failure of all efforts at land reform and redistribution which successive U.P. governments have carried out on paper, insufficient resources which the powerful have appropriated; corruption, armed bands of dacoits-bandits terrorising the poor, often in the pay of politicians and a police force demoralised, supine and corrupt. (Seabrook 1993: 34)

This passage summarizes some of the noteworthy features of the region, whose backwardness and resistance to development initiatives remains chronic. In this region, in which large landholdings have persisted despite zamindari abolition, landlords comprise not more than 5 per cent of the population, enjoying proprietary rights over 100-500 *bighas* (1 acre = 2.5 *bighas*). Even today in Tikariya and Jamunihai villages, over 3,000 *bighas* of *gaon samaj* lands are in the possession of erstwhile zamindars. Most landlords are of the Brahmin and Thakur castes, who have benefited more than they have lost as a result of land reform legislation, including legislation intended specifically for the landless. This has been done by registering the lands in the names of labourers traditionally attached to the landed families, without the accompanying intention of ever handing over the lands to them. Cultivation is carried out largely through crop-sharing arrangements, of which a variety exist in the region.

Day labourers receive *panchpahw* (1.25 kg. approximately) grain as daily wages. Alternatively, labourers receive daily wages (Rs. 20 for men and Rs. 15 for women) which are considerably lower than the prescribed minimum wage. As labourers are compelled to take loan advances from the landlords, a vicious cycle of bondedness emerges, the labourer being tied to the landlord until the loan is paid back, which is probably never.

The only option for survival among landless women appears to be the collection of firewood and its sale in neighbouring towns. The women calculated that the average number of days of paid work available to them in a year was not more than 40, hence firewood collection from neighbouring forests had emerged as a significant survival strategy for women. (Interview Gaindiya, Chitrakoot Dham). In this sense Kol and Chamar women of Banda represent prime examples of loss of control over productive resources and over the labour process and production.

Village Dadomafi illustrates the considerable ease with which erstwhile zamindars were able to appropriate surplus *gaon samaj* lands in the name of family members. With the connivance of obliging *patwaris* and *lekhpals*, it was possible for landlords to make fictitious transfers in the records and retain possession and occupancy. A result of this practice was that while a considerable number of *patta* deeds were issued, the real beneficiaries were unable to occupy the land. The beneficiaries belonging to the powerless

Kols and scheduled caste communities had documentary evidence of possession, but had no idea of the location of their holdings. It is within this context that the promise of land for the landless and the continuing landlessness and marginalization of these communities has to be understood. As I shall examine in the following section, landlessness further drove women of those groups into the clutches of acute forms of exploitation. There is an increasing disenchantment with the *patta* as a piece of paper instead of the much-desired rights over land. A landless woman of Manikpur remarked, 'it is the land we want rather than this piece of paper. Give us *kabza* over our lands'.

A characteristic feature of the villages of Manikpur block is the spatial dispersal of caste hamlets, which directly reflects the historical reality of feudal oppression and often its continued persistence until today. For instance, Rukmakhurd comprises neighbourhoods of fairly self-contained caste settlements which are also a substantial distance away from each other. Hamlets suggesting caste names such as Chamrori, Panditpurwa, Darziyan, Nayi Duniya and Bamhanipurwa have emerged as settlements away from the former village limits, as a result of caste groups moving away en bloc to escape zamindari oppressions.

Bundelkhand represents an area of extreme oppression particularly for members of the Kol tribe who are employed as agricultural labourers. In UP, unlike Madhya Pradesh, Kols are recognized as a Scheduled Caste, a fact which has serious consequences for their access to land. The classification has prevented them from benefiting from safeguards and facilities provided for tribes under the Constitution, a fact which has further marginalized the Kols. Amir Hasan, who made a study of three Kol villages in 1972, noted that 'the Kols being more primitive [*sic*], secluded and backward than other Scheduled Castes, have been put to disadvantage especially in the political field by their inclusion among Scheduled Castes' (Hasan 1972: 65). As landless labourers perceived as a Scheduled Caste without ancestral lands, the Kols find it increasingly difficult to establish claims over land or retain control over it. The literature on tribes has documented processes whereby aboriginal food gathering tribes were assimilated into the Hindu fold as Shudras or on the bottom rungs of the occupational hierarchy (Kosambi cited in Patnaik et al.: 3).

Traditional shifting cultivator tribal people have been integrated into a system of plough agriculture, thereby becoming an inferior subcaste in the Hindu hierarchy. Many acres of land formerly inhabited by the Kols have been sold in recent years in contravention of government regulations, which prohibit the sale of tribal lands to groups other than tribals. More recently 500 acres of Kol lands were sold to a private firm.

THE STORY OF *PATTAS* WITHOUT *KABZA*

14 people from our village gave money to the lekhpal for *pattas* of 5.5 *bighas* each. Over two years we have neither got the land nor has the money been returned.

In our village 50 pattas for Kol and Scheduled Caste families were made 20 years ago. Till today no one has come to measure the plots. People have occupied lands and are cultivating them. We request that the plots be measured out so that we are saved the hassle of running from pillar to post. (Radha Devi; Chamar caste, Harijanpur)

The rampant confusion with regard to the issue of *pattas* is evident in the following cases:

1. In Gobarhai village, the names of 72 Kols were registered in the *khatauni* as recipients of government *patta* lands. Out of these, 8 Kols were stated to be dead and against their names, Brahmins were entered as *waris* (heirs). Whenever the allottees, some of whom are women, have raised the issue of occupancy, they are threatened with death.
2. Indrakali, daughter of Bhadui Kol who was granted 5 *bighas*, got her land measured nine times but the influential occupier refused to return it. In 1994 in the Manikpur block *junta durbar*, the matter was raised for the ninth time, to no avail despite the pressure of Banda's administrative and police officials.
3. In *gram sabha* Saraiya, the blind son of the widow Chandi made unsuccessful attempts to occupy his 20 *bighas* of *patta* land for 18 years. In the process he claims to have spent Rs. 20,000 in fighting the case from the tehsil to the High Court.
4. In Diwariya, a Dom household was allotted a 6 *bigha* plot but the supposed recipients were not informed. When the family head, Raghuber, was asked for his thumb impression on a piece of paper, he made enquiries and found that the land was actually

registered in his name and that the occupiers were intending to obtain a bank loan for a pumping set.

5. In 1971, 23 Kols of Tikariya village, Karvi tehsil, were given 200 *bighas* of *patta* lands through the application of ceiling laws. The lands were originally in the proprietary possession of a Brahmin zamindar and MP. Until 1994 the *pattedars* had not received any land. They were told by the zamindar that the plots would be exchanged with the barren plots belonging to the *gaon sabha*. When the *lekhpal* began measuring his lands, he was roughed up, and when the Kols attempted to occupy the listed plots, they were threatened with rifles. On raising the question of rights, a youth was shot and killed. In such an intimidating atmosphere, women of the community felt that raising the issue of separate pattas for women is dangerous, and obtaining *pattas*, unlikely in the extreme (Pankaj 1996).

The cases above form the tip of the iceberg and draw attention to the thousands of acres in the name of Kols, which are still forcibly occupied by the powerful. In Sherihakhurd, the inhabitants of the Kolan (residential site of Kols in the village) assert that the fertility of their lands is the reason that 64 *bighas* have not yet been measured out to the different claimants and instead remain in the custody of the former landlords. Here it is said that owing to the rich soil and high wheat productivity, the established rural elite does not wish to part with the lands.

In village Jaromafi, 30 pattedars are unable to even identify their plots. Many are compelled to work as agricultural labourers on their own plots owing to the various legal loopholes which continually deprive them of their legitimate claims (Pankaj 1996: 2) In village Nihi, 165 *pattedars* have approximately 100 *bighas* in their names, but many are ignorant of this fact.

Two of the issues thrown up by these cases are the availability of lands for distribution, and the role of lekhpals and other local level government functionaries in the process of dispossession. The issues concern *gram sabha* land and lands declared surplus and then released after the implementation of land ceiling laws. All lands such as pasture, cultivable wasteland, and land under water, were vested with the *gram sabha* to be managed by the Land Management Committee at the village level. The lekhpal was the secretary of this body, presided over by the *pradhan*. Prior to 1969, the approval of the SDM was not necessary in order to allot any *gram sabha* land, and the writ of the lekhpal and pradhan was paramount (Shankar 1991: 5).

In colonial times, lekhpals were known as patwaris and wielded power as their entries in the land records were final and were upheld by the law courts. In the *khatauni*, the *patwari* could record the name of individuals to whom he decided that actual possession of land should be given, despite the fact that the land may in effect be under the proprietary possession of someone else. This power led to corruption, litigation and dispossession of rightful owners, and the erstwhile *patwaris* continued to wield their power as lekhpals in the post-Independence period (ibid.: 4).

An enquiry into the alarming problem of allotment of *gram sabha pattas* to other than the landless for the period 1 October 1964–1 August 1967 revealed that as many as 1.33 lakh *pattas* had been made contrary to the rules, and lekhpals had played a major role. As Section 198(2) of the Zamindari Abolition Act prevents the annulment of *pattas* after a lapse of three years, most of those made out to undeserving people during the first fifteen years of the Act were regularized. The further provision that someone can depose against the wrongful recipient of a government *patta* in order to annul it, also proved to be ineffective, as people were reluctant to depose against the powerful rural elite (ibid.: 5).

Thus, while many *pattas* were issued to those who were already landholders and kinsmen of erstwhile landed families, some did indeed come to the landless. But as the cases cited above reveal, many were awarded only in name, while actual control continued with others, or the previous owners. The Mangal Dev Visharad Committee found that out of 93 lakh acres of land vested with the *gaon sabha* in 1954, only 14 lakh acres were available for re-distribution among the landless. The remaining (and most fertile) lands had already passed into the hands of unauthorized persons through illegal encroachment as well as through substantial *pattas* granted by the Land Management Committees to recipients other than the landless. Out of the 14 lakhs available, 5.65 lakh acres were totally unfit for cultivation. Finally, after 1975 and under the '20-Point Programme', distribution of land among the landless received top priority and 8.5 lakh acres were distributed. Ironically, the most inferior lands were distributed among the most resourceless persons, which precluded investment on them (ibid.: 15).

The efforts of Indrakali and others to identify and measure their allotted lands point to the problems faced by women in gaining occupation of their *patta* lands. As boundaries are not demarcated, beneficiaries are dependent on the goodwill of the lekhpal and other functionaries. Where such lands are already under the occupation of others, bribery has become commonplace, and further disadvantages the landless as cash payments are beyond their means. In order to show that the process of allotment was accomplished, land was allotted on paper, without ascertaining whether it was occupied, or indeed whether the new allottee had managed to take possession of it.

In May 1989, the then Banda district magistrate asserted that by the end of that year, all Kols of Manikpur block would receive occupancy rights over their demarcated plots. A committee of eleven lekhpals was formed, and for one week work proceeded with enthusiasm; a hundred hectares were measured. However, owing to pressure from the rural power elite, the entire programme collapsed, and the team was withdrawn (Pankaj 1996: 4) In another such drive where the Kols' thumb impressions were required, the lists appeared with the imprints, but not a single plot had been measured or granted to the unsuspecting awardees. On further enquiry the Kols revealed that they were told that the list was a census enumeration paper, and hence had cooperated with their thumb impressions!

In tehsil Karvi, retired administrators assert that in the past ten years, there have been more than 5,000 cases of fraudulently acquired lands to the extent of 20,000 *bighas*. The market value of these is Rs. 65 crores. Owing to the land mafia, the files are returned to the record room with adequate stamps for sale, but in fact sales are never entered in the register. Instead, the registrar qanungo suppresses information. On countless occasions such files have been retrieved from the *peshkar's* cupboard, and it has been shown that they were never sent to Banda for processing.

To drag a case in court or to start a litigation is in the long run advantageous to the landlord as in the interim the malik's *kabza* on the land remains undisturbed while the poor *pattedar* is immediately dispossessed and helpless. The malik's court expenses are met by the produce from the very plots in dispute, while the landless have not the means or resources to engage in prolonged litigation (Pankaj 1987: 9). A complaint often heard in Banda was 'the landlords say, fight this battle in court, knowing that this would be seen as a taunt, a challenge few among the landless would ever knowingly take up'(1996: 4).

Thus *pattas* constituted fairly small or inadequate holdings; more often than not *pattas* had been issued on *banjar* or *usar* lands or on the *doob kshetra* (submerged part) of a river bank, disputed territory or forest land; very often there were more than two claimants on a single *patta*, leading to litigation and dispute. The problem of double entry was notorious in the region, often the first *patta*-holder being declared dead! Most disputes concerned those patta lands that landlords had released to meet the ceiling requirements, but which they continued to cultivate, and over which their occupancy as the power elite was firmly entrenched. In thousands of cases, the *patta* holders were in possession of the pieces of paper stating that the *patta* had been issued, yet were unaware of the location, so that twenty years may have passed, but the fields had not been measured or demarcated, nor the corresponding entries made in the village registers. The example of the *lekhpal's* attempts to measure the lands and consequent threats both to him and the Kols who were attempting to occupy them, explain the sense of futility experienced by many women.

WOMEN AS *PATTA* HOLDERS: PROBLEMS AND BIASES

When the state was unable to safeguard the *patta* rights of disadvantaged Kols, the situation was further compounded by administrative biases, which led to resistance to the idea of recognizing women as *patta* heirs.

In village Suargarh, Karvi Tehsil, Bhgirathi Kol had 46 *bighas* of agricultural land, which was occupied forcibly by Hiralal baniya. In 1958, the baniya with the connivance of the kanungo and lekhpal, was able to enter the land in the village register under the name of his minor son, Radheyshyam. The matter went to court and Hiralal lost consistenly until the case reached the Allahabad High Court. Meanwhile the Kol died and his wife, Duniya, who worked as an agricultural labourer, continued to fight the case. As payment for Duniya's court expenses, her husband's buffalo was auctioned.

On Duniya's death, her 5 daughters and an affinal nephew, Kalua, were entered as heirs (*waris*). Meanwhile, Hiralal acted once again and in collusion with officials, managed to enter his own name as waris in the records, on orders of the tehsildar. In 1990, Duniya's daughters manageed to get a stay against the tehsildar's order. Hiralal moved the Jhansi Commissionary to say that the SDO's court is not allowed to intervene on behalf of the daughters. Meanwhile Kalua, the affinal nephew, also died and Hiralal was now sole heir despite the fact that Kalua had four sons of his own. As the Kol women had obtained a stay order, they were entitled to occupy the land. The mustard crop, which they sowed on the land, was however harvested by Hiralal with the help of gun-toting goons. Protesting Kols were chased, locked up and prevented from the use of wells, ponds and roads of the village. While approximately 90 Kol women went to the thana to complain and seek justice, they were horrified to find that 12 fake cases had been registered against the Kol women and their husbands. (Pankaj 1996)

What is highlighted in this case is that the process of litigation involving agricultural land can take a lifetime. Also, the entire administrative machinery both at the village and tehsil levels is geared towards safeguarding the interests of the powerful. Here the lekhpal, kanungo and tehsildar supported a man's false claims, despite the obvious genuine ancestral claims of the Kols. In struggles regarding land, individual women are clearly at a disadvantage and can only be effective in united action. As Agarwal has pointed out, the building of group support among and for women, both locally and nationally, appears to be crucial for an effective struggle for land rights. As the most vulnerable among marginalized groups, women who are small cultivators and agricultural labourers are at an even greater disadvantage. The glimmerings of solidarity for collective action were in evidence though the modalities for subsequent action would depend on the maximization of class, caste and tribal interests with minimal areas of conflict. Finally, the case sensitizes us to the existence of significant differentiations within the class, in which people may own some land but also work for wages.

Two points are significant: in 1989 Duniya finally received the title to the land, a struggle which took over two decades, and denial of the use of roads, wells and ponds struck at the customary rights of women to common property resources, in a context where sustenance of families is largely woman's responsibility. The case raises significant questions about the manner in which the powerful within the village are able to deny the powerless their basic rights.

In the past, the village *wajib-ul-arz* usually laid down clearly and in detail the groups who had the right to the wood of dead trees, fruit, grass and firewood, the uses of ponds, *talabs* and wells, the village commons and roads; these were rights which could not be revoked, not even by the landlord. In the absence of such reference points, or with the deliberate suppression of such documents under new regimes, or wherever the complexity of tenurial and usufructuary rights in public lands such as forests and wastelands had not been worked out, the odds clearly appear to be loaded against the marginalized. For women in such situations, struggles to assert their rights to common resources must precede struggles to establish claims over *patta* lands.

BANJAR ZAMIN, *BANJH* WOMEN

Dhanya, dhanya Jhansi ki dharti
Dhanya dhanya woah pani
Dhanya Durge jisse durga sam
Pragati Laxmi rani.

Glory to the land of Jhansi,
glory to the climate
Glory to that garrison, from which emerged
(like Durga) the Rani of Jhansi.

R.H. Mitra, 1969, *Bundelkhand ki Sanskriti aur Sahitya*, Delhi: Rajkamal Prakashan (97)

The above lines, which permeate the folkore of the region, are synonymous with women's strength and empowerment. Women's reality is however a stark contrast to this empowering imagery. The evidence from Bundelkhand is particularly interesting as it allows for the exploration of linkages between the state's population policy (sterilization campaigns) which promised land to the landless. Tubectomy, linked to the crucial issue of land for women, emerged as an onslaught on their most fundamental constitutional rights. Grave questions about the government's population policies are raised because women of Scheduled Castes and tribal groups, the most marginalized sections of rural Banda, were the targets of the sterilization campaigns and the promise of *pattas.* The sense of betrayal still rankles among many of the women who for one reason or another, find their lands under dispute or occupied by others. For such women, the extreme step of sterilization, taken towards ensuring the economic security of families, has meant continued alienation from the state.

The etymological similarity between *banjar zamin* and *banjh* or barrenness has resulted in the use of the latter as a curse. Despite the acceptance of these parallels in popular usage, it is remarkable that only when women begin to assert their rights over the lands that their claims are ridiculed. As will be shown shortly, the women of Banda never got to establish control over the promised fields, yet were forced to relinquish control over their reproductive bodies.

I am the only heir of my parents. Though my father died four years ago, my name has not been entered as heir (*waris*) to my father's plot, though Halka lekhpal took Rs. 200 to make this entry two years ago. In addition, the lekhpal forced me and thirteen other women to get sterilized as a precondition for the reissuance of *pattas*. Our plots of 4.4 *bighas* had been measured out and we cultivated them for two years. Later, Godhan Singh from Unchadih and one Misra of Karvi dispossessed us of our lands. No action has been taken against them. (Aitwarya Kol, Village Hardiha, Thana Manikpur, Shahuji Nagar)

The consequences of government bias in viewing women as independent holders of land were in evidence particularly when women became recipients of *patta* lands only by virtue of their status as widows or through the dubious distinction of having submitted to a tubectomy during the government's drives for population control. As Agarwal points out, in the case of public land, women have to face the obstacle of male bias in land reform programmes, resettlement plans, and various development schemes. She found that government officials typically resist the allotment of public land to women on grounds that allotment can only be made to heads of households—who are assumed to be men (Agarwal 1994: 5).

I received a *patta* for an operation for birth control. Last year the *lekhpal* measured my plot of 5.5 *bighas*. I cleared, prepared and sowed the field. At harvest time I encountered thirty Kols in the field who prevented the harvesting. The Kols were armed with lathis and we exchanged abuses. Meanwhile the Thakur zamindar clan drove off in their tractor to the Karvi thana and registered a complaint against me. Then I received a summons from the police. The Kols were instigated by the zamindars—they are the zamindars' people.

Earlier when we were clearing the plot and preparing for cultivation, the zamindar did not say that the plot belonged to them. Now that we have made it cultivable, we are being threatened at gunpoint! We cannot fight against the Kols, for why should the poor fight each other? More than thirty Kols have also been given *pattas* in this area. We will not give up our plots—our papers are intact. [Ram Lali (Chamar), Harijanpur]

This incident hints at the strategies adopted by the rural elite to keep the landless poor divided. As both Kols and Chamars in Harijanpur are equal contenders for scarce resources, it is in the interests of village landholding groups to keep alive the contentious issue of undemarcated *pattas.* By delaying action on the measurement and demarcation of plots, the ex-landlords have continued to retain possession of their surplus lands as well as establish control over disputed *gaon sabha* lands, which were redistributed. A device followed by the landlords is to drag the case to court and then obtain a stay order, effectively putting a stop to cultivation on the plot for decades. It is women of the deprived groups who have found themselves needlessly drawn into such one-sided battles against the state, its legal machinery, and powerful rural elites.

My parents were bonded labourers of the former Sarpanch, Tegh Bahadur Singh. Taking advantage of my father's illiteracy, Tegh Bahadur Singh took a loan from the bank to purchase a pumpset in the name of my father. My parents are now dead, yet my name has not been entered in my father's plot of land. Though he died four years ago, later the lekhpal took Rs. 200 from me to make the entry two years ago. In addition he forced me and thirteen other women to get sterilized as a precondition for issuing *pattas*. The then DM had himself supervised the measuring out of 4 *bighas* to each of us and we were given occupancy. For two years we cultivated, but later the powerful Godhan Singh from Unchadih village and one Misra of Karvi forcibly dispossessed us. Until today no action has been taken against Tegh Bahadur Singh. When will I get justice? [Aitwarya (Kol) 34 years, Village Hardiha, Thana Manikpur, Shahuji Nagar]

The predominant motif captured in these accounts is the sense of betrayal experienced by women who submitted to the state's conditions for sterilization and then found themselves without land or any assurances for secure livelihoods. Women's powerlessness and lack of control over their lives and their bodies was reflected in the innumerable cases wherein women were promised *pattas* in lieu of sterilization. This linking of women's rights to land with an onslaught on their fundamental constitutional rights suggests a dubious history of women's rights, in addition to raising questions about government policies for women of Scheduled Castes and Tribes. In several cases, women had submitted to sterilization in return for house sites or low-income housing schemes offered by the Indira Awas Yojana. Ironically, owing to rampant corruption and poor quality of materials used, even these structures, received at considerable personal cost, are today reduced to rubble and remain unfit for habitation. In Rukmakhurd village, in fact, many such beneficiaries use these dilapidated structures as shelters for their pigs and goats.

BONDEDNESS AND INDEBTEDNESS

The Voices of Widows

In the following section a focus on bondage, a persistent form of precapitalist relations, is attempted. In the cases cited below, the dominant motif is the survival of feudal relations that allows institutions like bondage to survive and flourish. As land reforms were only partial, the exploitative relations of production remained intact with significant implications for the women involved. The link of bondedness with indebtedness is confirmed in these cases, which also force reflection on the vulnerability of widows and their resourcelessness in the patriarchal milieu.

1. My decased husband received a *patta* of 7 *bighas* approximately fourteen to twenty years ago. In his joy at becoming malik for the first time, he cleared the shrub, jungle, made the land cultivable and also harvested a good crop. The powerful of the village were unable to see this and planned a strategy to dispossess us the following year. When the field was being readied for sowing, Jagdish alias Bachai, Betai and Virendra of Tikariya village threatened us and occupied the land. Having become a widow I was unable to reclaim my land. I now live in Gadarpurwa and am forced to collect firehood and sell it in the bazar as this is my sole source of livelihood. (Buduwa, widow of Ramdev Motvan, Thana Markundi, Zilla Shahuiji Maharaj)

2. My husband's family were bonded labourers in the home of Baijnath Pandey. My husband Achelal was their *hulwaha* (ploughman). He was frequently beaten, and during my pregnancy he was made to disappear. Today my son is four years old but there is no sign of Achelal. After his disappearance I was oppressed in innumerable ways. Baijnath Pandey's son, Kesh Kumar Pandey, forced his attentions on me, frequently blocked my path and harassed me. My in-laws scolded me when I complained, and later the villagers advised me to leave the village and

return to my *maika.* When I took this step, my house was sold by Pandey to Ramji Kurmi and my 10 *bighas* of land was occupied by the village chowkidar Kori, and 4 *bighas* by the Pandeys. Today I have nothing and wonder if I can ever regain occupancy of my land and house. (Munni Kol, Village Kataiya Jhari,Thana and Zilla Allahabad)

3. My husband Binda Kol began cultivating 4 *bighas* of the *gaon samaj* lands in 1980, which he made cultivable through great effort. Hari Prasad, son of Dashrath, in connivance with the lekhpal managed to have the land entered in his own name after Binda's death. However, as the land was under my occupancy, I planted rice. Dashrath released cattle into the field and the entire crop was destroyed. On another occasion my crop was lifted from the threshing floor. Now they have registered a false case against me and oppression continues. (Rajkumari, Garha Katra, Shankargarh Thana, Zilla Allahabad)

4. I along with my husband worked as a bonded labourer of zamindar Keshav Tiwari. We received 5 *pav majdoori*. There were other bonded labourers working there twenty years ago. K. Tiwari took a bank loan of Rs. 40,000 each in the name of his bonded labourers to purchase a rifle. We did not know of this until the *vasuli* started coming for loan repayment. My husband was sent to jail on two occasions for this. On the third occasion, on hearing that they were coming to imprison him, he committed suicide. After his death, the lands in the name of my husband and father-in-law were forcibly occupied by K. Tiwari and he managed to enter them in his name, on the ground that our family must pay back the debt and loan. [Dujiya (Chamar), Hela]

5. I, Shivakalia and eight other Kol women were duped into putting a thumb impression on a blank piece of paper by the Pradhan, Amritlal Gadariya. He took a loan of Rs. 10,000 in each of our names. We did not know until the Amin repeatedly asked us to repay the loans. My husband became sick physically from worry and then died. We have not taken any loans and ask for justice.

Shiv Kalia	W/o Chotekona	Bargarh, Zilla Shahuji Nagar
Rukhmini	W/o Jugal Kishore	
Dhoklia	W/o Vishambar	
Surajkalia	W/o Hublal	
Nanki	W/o Sajan	
Duiji	W/o Golhe	
Ram Rati	W/o Ramsajivan	
Hirniya	W/o Ramlakhan	
Munni	W/o Nand Kishore	

6. My husband and I were bonded labourers of Pandit Khudiram. There were 14 *patta bighas* in my husband's name, which is occupied by Khudiram. On his death, Khudiram borrowed Rs. 1,000 on the basis of the land from an Unchadih bank, about which I came to know upon receiving the loan notice. Khudiram says I owe him Rs. 2,000 from the past and makes me do all the household chores and threatens me with death if I complain. He also threatens me with the gun. When will I get justice? [Lahuri, Sakroha village (Public Hearing on Kol Women, Delhi, 1997)]

These cases reveal the extent to which widows are particularly prone to unwanted attention by males. Sometimes this may be part of a larger strategy to drive out the widow from the village, enabling others to occupy her land and house. Coercion and pressure to give lands on *batai*, i.e. tenancy, for cultivation which can then be appropriated by the bataidar or lessee; the recurrent theme of loans in the names of bonded labourers; *pradhans* taking loans in the names of Kol widows where schemes have been started to benefit women and enable them to start small enterprises such as keeping goats, all point to the innumerable ways in which women remain vulnerable and marginalized.

It is in the crucial area of bondedness that the Kols of Banda have lost out as a result of their status as Scheduled Castes rather than Scheduled Tribes. The Scheduled Areas and Scheduled Tribes Commission had recommended that regulation be enacted for the cancellation of past debts and that regulations and restrictions be placed on moneylending. The tendency to extract *begar* in lieu of interest on loans advanced to Kols and the renewal of outdated and illegal pronotes has compounded the nature of the exploitation. A recommendation was made in 1972 that the state provide tribal people with loans even for non-productive purposes including the repayment of loans (Hasan 1972: 238). Until today there is little evidence of this having occurred. Rather, during fieldwork, as evidence of the deeply embedded chronic fear of *dadus* (landlords) the case of a Kol bonded labourer was cited, who was granted a sum of Rs. 5,000, at the initiative of an NGO to free him of his debt. The next morning the Kol returned the sum and went back to his *begar* because he suspected this was yet another ruse by the landlords to implicate him. Ironically, this single instance was cited as an example of the Kols' own preference for the 'good old days' and trust in the system of bonded labour and the security of the daily ration it provided.

For those who had *pattas* in 1972, the possibility of the land passing out of their hands to non-tribal people existed. State governments later issued an ordinance that land in the possession of SCs and STs is prohibited from being transferred to any but members of the same community. Despite this and prior to the passing of this ordinance, much land had already passed out of the hands of Kols. It is in the interests of landlords to prevent land redistribution as this will reduce the availability of cheap and bonded labour. Hence the resistance to getting *pattas* identified, measured and distributed.

The diverse aspects of bondedness and the exploitative employer-labourer relations within the rural population, which are further compounded in the case of women labourers, have already been seen. Clearly, since the castes in traditional bondage had been kept destitute and debarred from control of any means of production, taking advances against repayment through labour appeared to be the only survival option. In fact, small consumption loans appeared to have contributed to their bondedness. The evidence is startling for the fact that in several cases, the powerful managed to take loans in the names of their own bonded labourers!

A 1981 survey of bonded labour in Uttar Pradesh estimated that 10.40 per cent of the agricultural labour force is still bonded and 74 per cent of these belong to the Scheduled Castes, 14.2 per cent to the backward classes, and 7.40 per cent are Muslims (M. Sarma, 1981 cited in Chopra 1985: 167). The bonded labourers were predominantly landless or owned a negligible amount of land—68.30 per cent owned no land, 23.30 per cent had up to 1 acre and 4.40 per cent had between 1 and 2 acres. The majority, 93.50 per cent, were bonded because they had taken loans. Chopra's study of brick kiln workers in Muzaffarnagar suggests a link between agrarian and kiln bondage, as well as the fact that during the period the men are bonded, the women and children are exploited, purely on the basis of dependency.

> Bondage and pauperisation become a part of the life-cycle of the agricultural labourer after marriage, or after the birth of one or two children. This phenomenon is a part of the agrarian life-cycle, as evident from the fact that almost two-fifths of the respondents had been working on the kilns for over 15 years. (ibid.: 173)

These findings suggest that what begins as nominally free dependent labour slowly loses its nominal freedom over the years and declines into servitude, both in traditional industries like brick kilns and agriculture. It is clear that in the kiln at least, bondage is the traditional method of appropriating the labour of women and children as they become attached to dependent males during their life-cycles (ibid.: 174). Chopra noted that 87 per cent of the labourers surveyed were married, a fact which provided the owner access to the labour of their wives and children. The sample showed that out of the 339 male respondents, 332 were either married or had engaged the labour of a mother or daughter. Moreover, the respondents were vague regarding payment to the women and conceded that the wages to workers were paid to the man in charge of the working group.

Summing Up

Ka babi sab khatam ho gail?
Na mai, abhi ta surue bhaeel ba. (*Bhojpuri saying*)

So, is it all over, my fair one?
No, Ma, things have only just begun.

Women as a category are missing from most studies on agrarian society in India. Even enquiries into agrarian economy, and the nature of peasant consciousness and peasant movements, rarely take women into account. As subjects in their own right with agency or as significant contributors in agrarian production, women's invisibility remains a characteristic feature of Indian socio-historical studies. In the preceding pages I have foregrounded rural women in an effort to explore various dimensions of the problematic of their rights to land and its use. This exercise has been prompted by concerns which are academic as well as by implications for wider political questions of rural women's empowerment. I have tried to identify significant sources of powerlessness for women with a broad concern for the redressal of inequality and injustice arising from them. Underlying the enquiry, therefore, is the assumption that the legal title to land, access to it as a productive resource, and the ability to exercise control over it and enjoy the fruits of one's labour on it, have on the whole been denied to women.

This denial, to a large extent is responsible for the unequal gender equations within society and contributes to tilting power relations in favour of men and against women. As a corollary and conclusion of the enquiry, rural women's access to and control over land is seen not only as the single most empowering strategy in achieving gender parity and redressing existing power imbalances, but also in encouraging women's autonomy and decision-making while promoting economic independence, particularly where the very survival of families is dependent on women's roles and contributions.

In these pages I have sought to give visibility to women of various classes in the agrarian structure and particularly to their roles in production and their economic contributions. Here the assumption was that visibility will ensure recognition and awareness of the undervaluation of women's work, which is only the first step towards valuation and redressing structures of subordination, perhaps through eventual political action. Along with making women visible has been the attempt to uncover the biases and distortions in portraying women's reality. The foci on different classes and categories of women with their distinct interests, problems and needs prompted the conclusion that despite commonalities in the experience of broad gender oppressions, women have distinct and varied concerns and interests precisely due to their distinct locations within the relations of production. Hence, far from stressing their homogeneity, the areas of conflict between different classes and groups of women need acknowledgement.

Posing the question of how women got to be disenfranchised and distanced from ownership of land led to the exploration of certain hypotheses, which were tested against the available historical evidence. This dimension of the analysis was thus not an attempt at rewriting history but an effort at engaging with selected historical evidence which best illuminated the hypotheses. The enquiry has therefore worked at two levels—the identification of historical processes which have disenfranchised and disinherited women, and foregrounding women within certain historical processes and thus opening new ways of engaging with the past. With a distinct class of women within a given socio-economic formation as the central focus of each chapter, the impact of major societal processes on them could be assessed, allowing for a shift from generalities to particulars, which in turn gave way to the search for meaningful abstractions. Thus, for instance, the unintended impact of a colonial legislation on taluqdari women of Awadh served also to draw attention to ways in which women were kept out of its purview, a theme explored in subsequent chapters as well. Further, highlighting taluqdarins' predilections, strategies and (most importantly) their lack of control over land as well as the value it had for these women, allows for certain generalizations to emerge. In the absence of detailed gender-informed historical analyses of women within classes, the exercise concerning women of the landed elite acquires even greater significance, as it allows for comparisons and parallels to be drawn with women of other propertied classes.

I have also tried to show that the disenfranchisement of women from landed property always takes place along with the devaluation of their labour. It is not very difficult to see that had women's labour not been so devalued, they could probably have overcome the disenfranchisement with the hard labour they put into the household and field. Not being recompensed appropriately, despite the back-breaking jobs they do to make agriculture viable and feasible in the Indian countryside, has proved to be a double handicap for women. Historically, patriarchy and the state have been seen to be working in tandem to devalue women's labour.

As caste and class differentiate women, the various historical processes also differentially affect their rights to land and its produce. The life choices and strategies adopted by landless peasant women would differ from those of middle peasants or landowning groups. Devaluation of women's labour, for example, affected women of various classes differently. In a society where land is not merely a source of income but also a source of social authority/ power, status and cultural stability, owning land may also mean easy access to loans, respectability/dignity, and greater social mobility. Education, health, or other such social capital also become possible. And that means increased chances of better survival for themselves and their families.

As some of my findings indicate, women seem to adopt a two-pronged strategy in relation to rights over land. In the first case, acknowledging the norm of private ownership/private property relations, women are staking claims to joint ownership with men, as in the case of joint *pattas*. In the second case, in recognition of scarce resources, particularly lands for redistribution, women are concerned with strengthening collective control over village commons or *gram sabha* lands. They are recognizing the strength of collective action through *jan sangathans* where successful collective initiatives for land ownership and access to productive resources have led to their empowerment, hence drawing upon experiences from various parts of the country. The latter is a particularly useful strategy for women of the most marginalized groups, which constitute more than 60 per cent of the population engaged in agriculture. But until this becomes the dominant norm in society, women are not to forego joint ownership just because it underlines private property relations. It is not known whether they are aware of contradictions involved in pursuing this twin strategy, particularly when the Soviet model of development seems to have lost its appeal and the juggernaut of market forces rules the roost.

A myth that was exposed during fieldwork, was that rural women being illiterate, house-bound or less-intensely tied to the land, are unlikely to have considered opinions on the matter of land rights. To the contrary, women were found to be exceptionally well-informed even about the often complicated terms and conditions of tenancy arrangements. Wherever reluctance to share information with outsiders was observed, it usually stemmed from a perceived threat to the security of tenure, especially as the agrarian milieu of UP is characterized by concealed tenancy. In many cases women explained that there were only two ways in which they could gain access to land: *patta* ownership or concealed tenancy—and these were not mutually exclusive. First, for the landless or those with miniscule holdings, the distribution of *pattas* following the ceiling legislation of the 1970s had meant the possibility of the enitre household unit being able to utilize it as a productive resource. The second option wherein the peasant household entered into a lease arrangement with the landholder was based on verbal agreements for sharing the crop. In both cases, women recognized and sometimes lamented that they were seldom directly the *patta* owners or lessees, but that their productive activity was mediated through a senior male of the householding unit.

Women of marginalized households pointed out that in spite of the abundance of wage labour, landlords preferred to give lands on *batai*. This, they reasoned, implies that the responsibility for production which was taken by the bataidar's family collectively, far outweighed the advantage to the landlord which would accrue from personal supervision of labour. Where tenancy itself is concealed, the role of women within tenancy arrangements remains even more obscure. However, women's depth of information about the terms and conditions of their leases, reveals their own stakes in continuing livelihood security through *bataidari*.

Finally, perhaps no other culture places a greater premium on female fertility. Women are venerated as goddesses, as auspicious and fertile and a host of rituals relating to puberty and marriage reinforce female fertility. On the spiritual plane, the rituals serve to assuage and appease women, lulling them into a false sense of their centrality in creation. These notions however are rarely translated into the temporal plane, as landless women demanding equal shares in land have testified. The contradiction remains severe, as women continue to represent fertility and prosperity in the religious realm but must relinquish all rights to landownership. Rather, in several areas depending upon their locations, women found it hard even to conceive of owning land and the possibility of claiming land as a right seemed to many a remote possibility.

In this study I have tried to show that:

1. To know the peasant world it is important to know how peasant women relate to land. This relationship varies according to the caste and class locations of women.
2. Women's authority over land and their rights to own it are the key to their position in society.
3. Historical processes have worked towards keeping women away from meaningful rights over land.
4. To empower rural women it is crucial to ensure them secured access to productive resources.
5. The focus of enquiry into women's rights to land has to shift away from individual to collective ownership.

Appendices

APPENDIX I

Government Gazette UP, 15 October 1986

"Whereas the areas held or acquired by educational institutions for purposes of instruction and buildings were . . . declared by the Governor under clause c of sub-section 1 of section 2 of the Uttar Pradesh Zamindari Abolition and Land Reforms Act 1950 to the areas held or occupied for a public purpose or a work of public utility, and were as such exempted from the operation of the said Act;

And whereas the Governor is, further, satisfied that it will not be in the public interest to allow continuance of the said exemption in respect of the said areas of the State covered by the said notification of July 1, 1952;

Now, therefore, in exercise of the powers under sub-section 3 . . . the Governor is pleased to appoint October 15, 1986 as the date on, and with effect from which the said Act shall come into force in the said areas."

Sd. Mohinder Singh (Sachiv)
(*Government Gazette*, U.P. Extraordinary,
Vidhayi Parishisht, 15 October 1986-document)

APPENDIX II

Provisions of Land Acquisition Act, 1894

The Act which was enacted in 1894 for the acquisition of land for public purposes also had provisions which spelt out the amount of compensation to be made for such acquisitions.

a. It stated that wherever it appears to the appropriate government that land in any locality is needed for any public purpose, a notification to that effect shall be published in the Official Gazette as well as through other public notices.

b. The Act made it lawful for government officials to enter and survey the land, to dig and bore in the subsoil to ascertain the suitability of the land for the intended purpose as well as to set out the boundaries of the land proposed to be taken.

c. Any damage at the time of the entry was to be paid for and in case of dispute with regard to the sufficiency of the amount, the government officer was to refer the dispute to the Collector or Chief Revenue Officer of the district.

d. Objections to acquisition of the stated land for public purposes by a person interested in the land had to be submitted to the Collector in writing within 30 days. The government would then make its recommendations on the objections and government's decision on the objections was to be treated as final.

e. Only such a person was deemed to be interested in the land (in the clause above) who would be entitled to claim an interest in compensation if the land were acquired under this Act.

f. After the issuing of public notices regarding government intentions with regard to the land, claims to compensation for all interests in such land were to be made to the Collector, both in person and in writing. The Collector could also serve notice on the occupier of the land.

g. Information on interests in the land of co-proprietor, sub-proprietor, mortgagee, tenant etc. and the nature of their interests, of rents and profits receivable by them for the next three years were to be elicited for purposes of compensation.

h. At an appointed time, not exceeding a period of two years from the date of publication of notification, the Collector was authorised to award compensation to interested persons.

i. The collector had the power to summon witnesses, to requisition documents etc. for purpose of enquiries under the Act.

j. After making the compensation award, the collector could take possession of the land which would then vest absolutely in the government free of all encumbrances.

k. Within 6 weeks of the date of the Collector's award, individuals who did not accept the award on whatever grounds , could apply in writing to the Collector in order that the matter be determined by the court. Objections could range from measurement of land, amount of compensation, to whom it is to be paid, or the apportionment of the compensation among the persons interested.

l. In determining compensation, factors to be taken into account included, the market value of the land; the damage sustained by the interested person e.g. standing crops or being compelled to change his residence or business. (*Land Acquisition Act, 1894*. Eastern Book Company 1992, Lucknow)

Glossary

Akhara	Gymnasium
Amin	Revenue functionary primarily one who measures land.
Annadaan	Offering of food for religious merit.
Anuloma	Socially accepted marraige or union, usually hypergamous, wife-givers being subordinate in status to wife-takers.
Asarh	Fourth month of the Hindu solar year, June-July, the rainy season and the beginning of rice cultivation.
Avatar	Incarnation
Baniya	Merchant, traders, moneylending caste
Banjar	Barren
Barat	Bridegroom's marriage procession
Batai	Peasant's sharecropping arrangements with landlords
Bataidar	Tenant
Bhajan	Religious song
Bhomia	Land grantee of a unit called 'bhom' in Rajasthan
Bigha	A measure of land which is approximately five-eighth of an acre.
Biswa	1/20th part of a *bigha* unit of measurement
Burra Thakur	Elder or senior Rajput landlord
Chapperband	Homestead
Chathi	Sxith day after birth
Daan	Offering made to earn religious merit
Dadu	Local term for oppressive landlord in Bundelkhand region
Doob khsetra	Submerged part
Farman	State order or edict

Gadari	Wooden bobbin on which ropes used for drawing water from wells are wound
Gaddee	Throne; primogeniture, seat
Gagra	Earthenware pot
Grihastha	Middleman
Hasiya	Sickle
Hissedars	Shareholders
Hukka	Hubble Bubble or pipe in which tobacco is smoked
Hulwaha	Ploughman
Jagir.	Land of which revenue was made over to an individual usually as payment of service
Jajmani	System of exchange of produce and services in a patron-client relationship
Janeo	Sacred thread worn by twice-born castes
Julaha	Weaver
Junta durbar	Public hearing
Jurabant	Principles for the division of property among offspring from several wives
Kabza	Occupation; control or occupancy
Kanungo	Land Inspector (Revenue Officer)
Kartik	Eighth Hindu month, October-November
Kayer	Harness for bullocks
Kharif	Autumn, autumnal crop
Khasra	Field register
Khatauni	Field records
Khurpi	Small hand hoe
Kiaris	Division of fields into beds with raised borders to facilitate irrigation
Kudar	Sharp pointed axe
Kutcherry	Court
Lathi	Stave, stick
Lekhpal	Revenue clerk incharge of maintaining revenue records
Lota	Metal water pot
Maika	Woman's natal home
Mardana	Space set apart for male interaction or work, hence out of bounds for women
Mohalla	Colony, neighbourhood
Mundan	First tonsure

Naar	Thick rope used for drawing water from wells
Natakshala	Theatre/auditorium
Nazrana	Present or premium given by tenant to landlord; also gift
Pattas	Deeds of lease; documents specifying conditions on which lands are held
Panchayats	Village level council for judicial purposes; lowest level local administrative body
Panchpaw	1.25 kgs.
Pat	Form of marriage popular among low castes
Patha	Stony
Pativrata dharma	Devotion to husband with premium on chastity and fidelity
Pattedars	Holders of pattas or title deeds to land
Patwaris	Revenue functionary for revenue collection, fixing of land rent; village accountant
Peshkar	Court Clerk
Phaoris	Spades
Pradhan	Headman
Pratiloma	Unions against the grain, socially unacceptable usually hypogamous
Purohit	Priest who conducts religious ceremonies
Rabi	Spring or spring harvest where the crop is sown after the rains and reaped in the first three or four months of the year
Rais	Wealthy person
Riyasat	Princely-estate
Sanad	Title deeds conferred in Awadh by the British on selected members of the former landed elite after 1857
Sanatan dharma	core of religious beliefs and practices from time immemorial, i.e. before institutionalized religion
Shikmi	Sub-tenant
Shuddhi	Purification
Sipahi	Soldier
Soup	Angular basket for tossing grain to separate impurities
Taluqa	Estates owned by taluqas and conferred through Sanad

Taluqdars	Possessors of estates, often owners of small principalities
Taravad	Nayar estate inherited matrilineally
Tehsil	Administrative subdivision
Tehsildar	Head of administrative subdivision
Thali	Metal plate or dish for meals
Thana	Subordinate police outpost
Tilak	Ceremonial mark on forehead applied on various auspicious occasions
Usar	Barren
Varnasamkara	Theory of four orders or varnas
Vasuli	Recovery of dues
Wajib-ul-arz	Record of rights. Record of duties and obligations of village population
Waqf	Endowment
Waris	Heir
Yagnopavit	Post-puberty initiation rites for commencement of use of sacred thread among twice-born caste boys
Yajman	Patron
Yuvraj	Scion of a royal lineage, usually heir of landed estate
Zari	Weaves of gold or silver threads
Zenana	Space set apart for women to reside, work, etc., prohibited for men
Zilledar	Collector of rent for an estate

Bibliography

Agarwal, Bina, 1995. 'Gender and Legal Rights in Agricultural Land In India', *Economic and Political Weekly*, 25 March.

———, 1995. *A Field of One's Own*, Delhi: Cambridge University Press.

———, 1994. *Gender and Command Over Property: An Economic Analysis of South Asia*, Delhi: Kali for Women.

Agnihotri, Indu, 1996. 'Bringing Land Rights Centre-Stage', *EPW*, 2 March 1996.

Asif, M., 1999. 'Land Acquisition Act: Need for an Alternative Paradigm', *EPW*, 19 June.

Baba Ramchandra Papers, 1933-50. Delhi: Nehru Memorial Museum & Library.

Bahadur, K.P. (ed.), 1978. *History, Caste and Culture of Rajputs*, Delhi: ESS Publications.

Banerjee, N., 1999. 'Analysing Women's Work under Patriarchy', in K. Sangari and U. Chakravarti (eds.), *From Myths to Markets: Essays on Gender*, Delhi: Manohar.

———, 1996. 'The Structural Adjustment Programme and Women's Economic Empowerment', in N. Rao, L. Rurup and R. Sudarshan (eds.), *Sites of Change: The Structural Context for Empowering Women in India*, FES and UNDP, New Delhi.

Bankelal, Lala, 1909. *Kanyamanoranjan*, Moradabad: Lakshminarayan Press.

———, 1909. *Naarisudasha Pravartak*, Moradabad: Lakshminarayan Press.

Bhadani, B.L. (ed), 1980. *Administration of the Bikaner State in the 17th Century*, Bikaner.

Bhargava, Meena. 1996. 'Landed Property Rights in Transition: A Note on Cultivators and Agricultural Labourers in Gorakhpur in the Late 18th and 19th Century', *Studies in History* (n.s.) 12 (2).

Bhattacharya, Neeladri. 1985. 'Agricultural Labour and Production:

Central and South-East Punjab 1870-1940', in K.N. Raj, N. Bhattacharya, S. Guha and S. Padhi (eds.), *Essays on the Commercialisation of Indian Agriculture,* Delhi: Oxford University Press.

Bilgrami, R.A., 1989. 'Muslim Women and Land Grants', paper presented at CWDS National Seminar on Women and Access to Land and Productive Resources, University of Delhi.

———, 1984. *Religious and Quasi-Religious Departments of the Mughal Period (1556-1707)*, Delhi: Munshiram Manoharlal.

Boserup, E., 1970. *Women's Role in Economic Development,* London: George Allen & Unwin Ltd.

———, 1990. 'Economic Change and the Roles of Women', in I. Tinker (ed.), *Persistent Inequalities: Women and World Development,* New York: Oxford University Press.

Brara, R., 1994. 'Kinship and the Political Order: The Afghan Sherwani Chiefs of Malerkotla (1454-1947)', *Contributions to Indian Sociology* (n.s.), 28/2.

Brass, Tom, 1993-4. 'Introduction: The Politics of Gender: Nature and Nation in the Discourse of the New Farmers Movements', *Journal of Peasant Studies,* 21.

Breman, Jan, 1979. *Patronage and Exploitation: Changing Agrarian Relations in South Gujarat*, Delhi: Manohar.

Breman, J. and S. Mundle (eds.), 1991. *Rural Transformation in Asia,* Delhi: Oxford University Press.

Brown, Judith K., 1970. 'A Note on the Division of Labor by Sex', *American Anthropologist 72.*

Census Report, 1931. 'Some Ethnographical Notes on Castes and Tribes', Government Press.

Chakravarty, U., 1998. *Rewriting History: The Life and Times of Pandita Ramabai,* Delhi: Kali for Women.

Childe, G., 1976. *What Happened in History?* London: Penguin.

Chandhoke, N., 1994. 'Why People Should Have Rights', *EPW,* 8 October.

Chandra, S., 1974. 'Some Aspects of Indian Village Society in N. India during 18th Century', *Indian Historical Review*, vol. 1/1, March.

Chowdhry, P., 1995. 'Contesting Claims and Counter Claims: Questions of the Inheritance and Sexuality of Widows in a Colonial State', *Contributions to Indian Sociology* (n.s.), 29, 1&2.

———, 1995. *The Veiled Women: Shifting Gender Equations in Rural Haryana, 1889-1990*, Delhi: Oxford University Press.

———, 1997. 'Enforcing Cultural Codes: Gender and Violence in Northern India', *EPW*, 10 May.

Collier, J.F. and S.J. Yanagisako, 1987. 'Toward a Unified Analysis of Gender and Kinship', in Collier and Yanagisako (eds.), *Gender and Kinship: Essays Toward a Unified Analysis*, Stanford, California: Stanford University Press.

Cooper, J.P., 1976. 'Patterns of Inheritance and Settlement by Great Landowners from 15th to the 18th Centuries', in J. Goody, J. Thirsk and E.P. Thompson (eds.), *Family and Inheritance*, Cambridge: Cambridge University Press.

Crooke, W., 1975. *Tribes and Castes of N.W. India*, vols. II and III (rpt), Delhi: Cosmo Publications.

Dingwaney, M. and U. Patnaik (eds.), *Chains of Servitude, Bondage and Slavery in India*, Delhi: Sangam Books.

Dreze, J. and H. Gazdar, 1995. 'Uttar Pradesh: The Burden of Inertia', J. Dreze and A. Sen (eds.), *Indian Economic Develop-ment and Social Opportunity*, Delhi: Oxford University Press.

———, 1998. *Indian Development: Selected Regional Perspectives*, Delhi: Oxford University Press.

Dube, L., E. Leacock and S. Ardener (eds.), 1986. *Visibility and Power: Essays on Women in Society and Development*, Delhi: Oxford University Press.

Evans-Pritchard, E.E., 1965. *The Position of Women in Primitive Society and Other Essays in Social Anthropology*, London: Faber and Faber.

Fernandes, Walter, 1998. 'Land Acquisition (Amendment) Bill 1998: Rights of Project-Affected People', *EPW*, October.

Fisher, E., 1979. *Women's Creation*, New York: Anchor Press.

Fox, R.G., 1971. *Kin, Clan, Raja and Rule*, Bombay: Oxford University Press.

Gilmartin, D., 1981. 'Kinship, Women and Politics in Twentieth Century Punjab', in Gail Minault (ed.), *The Extended Family: Women and Political Participation in India and Pakistan*, Delhi: Chanakya.

Goody, J., 1976. 'Inheritance, Property and Women: Some Comparative Considerations', in J. Goody, J. Thirsk and E.P. Thompson (eds.), *Family and Inheritance*, Cambridge: Cambridge University Press.

Hirschorn K. (ed.), 1984. *Women and Property—Women as Property*, London: St. Martin's Press.

Goody, Jack, John Thirsk and E.P. Thompson (eds.), 1976. *Family and Inheritance*, Cambridge: Cambridge University Press.

Government Gazette, 1986. U.P. Extraordinary, Vidhayi Parishisht, 15 October.

Habib, Irfan, 1963. *The Agrarian System of Mughal India (1556-1707)*, Bombay: Asia Publishing House.

Hasan, A., 1972. *The Kols of Patha*, Allahabad: Kitab Mahal.

Herring, R.J., 1983. *Land to the Tiller: The Political Economy of Agrarian Reform in South Asia*, Delhi: Oxford University Press.

Ibbetson, D.C.J., 1983. *Report on the Census in Punjab, 1881.*

Lerner, G., 1986. *The Creation of Patriarchy*, New York: Oxford University Press.

Jafri, S.N.A., 1931. *The History and Status of Landlord and Tenant in the United Provinces* (rpt), Delhi: Usha, 1985.

Jaiswal, S. 1997. 'Tribe, Caste Interaction: A Reexamination of Certain Issues', in D. Nathan (ed.), *From Tribe to Caste*, Shimla: Indian Institute of Advanced Study.

Jaiswal, S., 1998. *Caste: Origin, Function and Dimensions of Change*, Delhi: Manohar.

Jassal, Smita Tewari, 1980. 'Agrarian Contradictions and Resistance in Faizabad District of Oudh (India) 1858-1970', *Journal of Peasant Studies*, vol. 7, no. 3.

———, 1988. 'Agrarian Structure: A Study of the Faizabad District', unpublished Ph.D. thesis, Department of Sociology, Delhi University.

Jayaswal, G.P., 1928. 'Rajapuri Brahmanon ke Naam Khuli Chitthi', Dumraon: Thatheri Bazar, Shahabad, 15 July.

Karve, I., 1964. *Kinship Organisation in India*, Bombay: Asia Publishing House.

Klass, M., 1998. *Caste: The Emergence of the South Asian Social System*, Delhi: Manohar.

Kosambi, D.D., 1975. *An Introduction to the Study of Indian History*, Bombay: Popular Prakashan.

Patnaik, Utsa, 1985. 'Introduction', in M. Dingwaney, U. Patnaik (eds.), *Chains of Servitude, Bondage and Slavery in India*, Delhi: Sangam Books.

Kozlowski, G.C., 1985. *Muslim Endowments in British India*, Cambridge: Cambridge University Press.

———, 1989. 'Muslim Women and Control of Property in North India', in J. Krishnamurty (ed.), *Women in Colonial India: Essays on Survival, Work and the State*, Delhi: Oxford University Press.

Kulke, H., 1993. *Kings and Cults: State Formation and Legitimation in India and Southeast Asia*, Delhi: Oxford University Press.

Kumar, A., 2001. *Language of Politics*, forthcoming, Delhi: Manohar.

Kumar, Kapil, 1989. 'Rural Women in Oudh, 1917-47: Baba Ramchandra and the Women's Question', in K. Sangari and S. Vaid (eds.), *Recasting Women: Essays in Colonial History*, Delhi: Kali for Women.

Lal, C.B., 1942. *Taluqdari Law of Awadh*, Allahabad.

Land Acquisition Act, 1894, 1992. Lucknow: Eastern Book Company.

Landes, Joan B., 1988. *Women and the Public Sphere in the Age of the French Revolution*, Ithaca: Cornell University Press.

Leacock, E., 1974. Review of Steven Goldberg's, 'The Inevitability of Patriarchy', *American Anthropologist*, LXXVI, no. 2.

Leacock, E. and M. Etienne, 1980. 'Introduction', in E. Leacock and M. Etienne (eds.), *Women and Colonization: Anthropological Perspectives*, New York: Praeger.

Leacock, E., 1986. 'Woman, Power and Authority', in L. Dube, E. Leacock and S. Ardener (eds.), *Visibility and Power: Essays on Women in Society and Development*, Delhi: Oxford University Press.

———, 1978. 'Women's Status in Egalitarian Society: Implications for Social Evolution', *Current Anthropology*, vol. 19, no. 2, June 1978.

Leacock, E. and M. Etienne (eds.), 1980. *Women and Colonization: Anthropological Perspectives*, New York: Praeger.

Lerche, J., 1995. 'Is Bonded Labour a Bound Category? Reconceptualising Agrarian Conflict In India', *The Journal of Peasant Studies*, vol. 22, no. 3.

Lerner, G., 1986. *The Creation of Patriarchy*, New York: Oxford University Press.

Levi-Strauss, C., 1968. *Structural Anthropology*, London: Allen Lane.

Ludden, David, 1985. *Peasant History in South India*, New Jersey: Princeton.

Lyall, A., 1884. *Asiatic Researches:Religious and Social*, London: John Murray.

Mehta, Deepak, 1997. *Work, Ritual, Biography: A Muslim Community in North India*, Delhi: Oxford University Press.

Metcalfe, Thomas R., 1979. *Land, Landlords and the British Raj—Northern India in the Nineteenth Century*, Delhi: Oxford University Press.

Mazumdar, V., 1997. 'Peasant Women, Land Rights and Agricultural Development Perspectives from the Indian Women's Movement', in N. Rao and L. Rurup (eds.), *A Just Right, Women's Ownership of Natural Resources and Livelihood Security*, Delhi: FES.

Meillassoux, C., 1981. *Maidens, Meals and Money*, Cambridge: Cambridge University Press.

Menon, A.G., 1996. 'Re-Negotiating Gender: Enabling Women to Claim Their Right to Land Resources', paper presented at Special Event: Women's Legal Rights to Land/Property, held at the NGO Forum (Habitat II), UN Conference on Human Settlements—Habitat II, Istanbul, June.

Mies, M., 1982. *The Lacemakers of Narsapur: Indian Housewives Produce for the World Market*, London: Zed Press.

———, 1988. 'Social Origins of the Sexual Division of Labour', in M. Mies et al. (eds.), *Women—The Last Colony*, Delhi: Kali for Women.

Mies, M. et al. (eds.), 1988. *Women—The Last Colony*, Delhi: Kali for Women.

Millett, A.F., 1921. Report on the Land Revenue of the Fyzabad District. NWP, Allahabad and Oudh Government Press.

Minault, Gail (ed.), 1981. *The Extended Family: Women and Political Participation in India and Pakistan*, Delhi: Chanakya.

'Mitra', Ramcharan Hayaran, 1969. *Bundelkhand ki Sanskriti aur Sahitya*, Delhi: Rajkamal Prakashan.

D.N., 1988. 'A Land Struggle', *EPW*, 5 March.

Nathan, Dev, 1996, 'Agricultural Labour and the Poor Peasant Movement in Bihar', in T.V. Sathyamurthi (ed.), *Class Formation and Political Transformation in Post Colonial India*, Delhi: Oxford University Press.

———, 1997, 'Gender Transformation in Tribes', in D. Nathan (ed.), *From Tribe to Caste*, Shimla: Indian Institute of Advanced Study.

Nevill, H.R. 1905. *Fyzabad: A Gazetteer*, Allahabad: Government Press.

Oudh Cases, vol. XIV, 1911. '*Nazir Ahmed* vs. *Swami Dayal*, etc. November 27'.
Oudh Cases, vol. XV, 1912.
Oudh Cases, vol. XXI, 1916.
Oudh Cases, 1917. '*Bisheshwar Baksh Singh* vs. *Rameshwar B. Singh*', 6 July.
Oudh Cases, vol. XXV, 1921, '*Jai Indra Bahadur Singh* vs. *Rani Bijai Raj Kooer*'.
Oudh Cases, vol. XXIX, no. 73, 1924.
Oudh Cases, vol. XXVIII, 1924, '*Babu Achai Singh* vs. *Babuain Shangunath Koer*'.
Oudh Cases, vol. XXVIII, 1924, '*Wazir Mohammad* vs. *Har Pershad*'.
Pankaj, H.S., 1996. *Dharti ka Dard*, Manikpur: Akhil Bharatiya Samaj Sewa Sansthan, 15 August.
———, 1987. 'Land Reforms—Myth and Reality', *Yojana*, 16-31 December.
Palriwala, R. and C. Risseeuw (eds.), 1996. *Shifting Circles of Support*, Delhi: Sage Publications.
Patnaik, U. 1991. 'Ascertaining the Economic Characteristics of Peasant Classes in Themselves in Rural India: A Methodological and Empirical Exercise', in J. Breman and S. Mundle (eds.), *Rural Transformation in Asia*, Delhi: Oxford University Press.
———, 1976. 'Class Differentiation within the Peasantry: An Approach to the Analysis of Indian Agriculture', *EPW*, vol. XI, no. 39.
———, 1987. *Peasant Class Differentiation: A Study in Method with Reference to Haryana*, Delhi: Oxford University Press.
Pawar, Krishnashankar, 1933. *Kurmi-jati Nirnaya*, Delhi: Kshatriya Research Society.
Pinch, W., 1996. *Peasants and Monks in British India*, Delhi: Oxford University Press.
Plunkett, Frances T., 1973. 'Royal Marriages in Rajasthan', in *Contributions to Indian Sociology* (n.s.), (64-80).
Poitevin, G. and H. Rairkar, 1993. *Indian Peasant Women Speak Up*, Bombay: Orient Longman.
Poulantzas, N., 1978. *State, Power, Socialism*, London: New Left Books.
———, 1979. *Fascism and Dictatorship*, London: Verso.
Public Hearing on Kol Women, 4 November 1997, Mavalankar Auditorium, New Delhi.
Rai, S., 1996. 'Women and the State in the Third World: Some Issues

for Debate', in S. Rai and G. Lievelsky (eds.), in *Women and the States: International Perspective,* London: Taylor and Francis.

Ramanathan, U., 1995. 'Displacement and Rehabilitation: Towards a National Policy', *Lokayan Bulletin,* 11: 5.

Randall, V. and G. Waylen, 1998. *Gender Politics and the State,* London: Routledge.

Rao, M.S.A., 1979. *Social Movements and Social Transformation: A Study of Two Backward Class Movements in India,* Delhi: Macmillan.

Rao, N. and K. Rana, 1997. 'Land Rights and Women: Case of Santhals', *EPW,* 7 June.

Rao, N. and L. Rurup (eds.), 1997. *A Just Right. Women's Ownership of Natural Resources and Livelihood Security,* Delhi: FES.

Reddy, N., 1991. 'Why is Land Reforms Not a Non-Issue?', National Workshop on Impact of Land Reforms, Mussoorie: Lal Bahadur Shastri Academy of Administration (unpublished).

Risley, H.H., 1892, *The Tribes and Castes of Bengal,* vol. I. Calcutta: Bengal Secretariat Press.

Rosaldo, M.Z. and L. Lamphere, 1974. *Women, Culture and Society,* Stanford: Stanford University Press.

Roy, S., 1908. *Customs and Customary Law in British India,* Tagore Law Lectures, Delhi: Mittal Publication, 1986 (rpt.).

Sacks, K., 1979. *Sisters and Wives: The Past and Future of Sexual Equality,* Connecticut: Westport.

Sangari, Kumkum and Sudesh Vaid (eds.), 1989. *Recasting Women: Essays in Colonial History,* Delhi: Kali for Women.

Sardamoni, K., 1996. 'Women's Rights and the Decline of Matriliny in Southern India', in R. Palriwala and C. Risseeuw (eds.), *Shifting Circles of Support*, Delhi: Sage Publications.

Sarma, M., 1981. 'Bonded Labour in India', National Survey on the Incidence of Bonded Labour, Final Report.

Sarvekshna. October-December 1995.

Satyamurthi T.V. (ed.), 1996. *Class Formation and Political Transformation in Post-Colonial India,* Delhi: Oxford University Press.

Scott, Joan and Louise A. Tilly, 1975. 'Women's Work and Family in Nineteenth Century Europe', *Comparative Studies in Society and History* 17.

Seabrook, J., 1993. *Notes From Another India,* London: Pluto Press.

Sen, Samita, 1999. *Women and Labour in Late Colonial India the Bengal Jute Industry*, Cambridge: Cambridge University Press.

Shankar, K., 1991. *Some Aspects of Land Distribution Programme in U.P.*, Allahabad: G.B. Pant Social Science Institute.

Sharma, Miriam, 1985. 'Caste, Class and Gender: Production and Reproduction in N. India', *Journal of Peasant Studies*, vol. 12, no. 4, July.

Sharma, R.S., 1983. *Material Culture and Social Formation in Ancient India.* Delhi: Macmillan.

Sharma, U., 1976. 'Status Striving and Striving to Abolish Status', *Social Action*, vol. 26, July-September.

Singh, C., 1988. 'Conformity and Conflict: Tribes and the Agrarian System of Mughal India', *Indian Economic and Social History Review*, 23/3.

Singh, K.S., 1994. *The Scheduled Tribes*, vol. III, Anthropological Survey of India, Delhi: Oxford University Press.

Singh, Shri Durgashankar Prasad, 1958. *Bhojpuri ke Kavi aur Kavya*, Patna: Bihar Rashtrabhasha Parishad.

Srinivas, M.N., 1996. *Village, Caste, Gender and Method in Essays in Indian Social Anthropology*, Delhi: Oxford University Press.

Swaminathan, M.S., 1985. 'The Role of Education and Research in Enhancing Rural Women's Insurance and Household Happiness', First J.P. Naik Memorial Lecture, New Delhi: CWDS.

Thompson, E.P., 1976. 'The Grid of Inheritance', in Jack Goody, John Thirsk and E.P. Thompson (eds.), *Family and Inheritance*, Cambridge: Cambridge University Press.

Thukral, E.G., 1996. 'Development, Displacement and Rehabilitation: Locating Gender', *EPW*, 15 June.

Tod, James, 1832. *Annals and Antiquies of Rajasthan*, vols. 1 and 2, Delhi: MN Publishers (rpt., 1983).

Trautmann, T.R., 1981. *Dravidian Kinship*, Cambridge: Cambridge University Press.

Whitehead, A., 1984. 'Women and Men; Kinship and Property: Some "General issues"', in K. Hirschorn (ed.), *Women and Property—Women as Property*, London: St. Martin's Press.

Waylen, G. 1998. 'Gender, Feminism and the State', in V. Randall and G. Waylen (eds.), *Gender Politics and the State*, London: Routledge.

Index

Agarwal, Bina 17, 19-21, 35, 108, 147, 158, 160
Agnihotri, Indu 145
agrarian class 11
agrarian relations, inequities in 17
agrarian societies, power structure in 145
agrarian structure, legislative impact on 88
agricultural castes 52-3
agricultural labourers 12-13, 20, 47
agriculture, women involvement in 34
agriculture growth, and gender relations 45-6
Akbar 116-17
All India Yadava Mahasabha 53
Anath Ablaon ki Pukar 83
arable land 13, 17
Arya Samaj 50, 53, 59-60
Asif, M. 125
Aurangzeb 116, 118
Awadh Taluqdari Succession Act of 1869 88-9, 92, 94-5, 101-5, 110
  implications for women 102-5
  social implications of 89
  taluqdar responses to 101-2

Bahadur, K.P. 99-100
Babu Achai Singh vs. *Babuain Shangunath Koer* 94
band societies, ethnographic analysis 38-40
banjar barren land 132, 157, 159-62
Banerjee, Nirmala 33, 142
banjh women 159-62
bataidari 170
begari 83-5, 164
benevolent paternalism, state of 121
Bhadani 108
Bhargava 72, 74
Bhattacharya 65
Bilgrami, R.A. 116
Birhor of Jharkhand, communal forms among 40-1
Boserup, E. 36
Brara, R. 96-7, 100
Brass, Tom 66
Breman, Jan 65
Brijraj Koer vs. *Mahadeo Baksh* 101
British India Association (BIA) 106, 108-9

Capper 82
caste,
  adulterous low-caste women 120
  and classes, 15
  and kinship codes enforcement in rural Haryana 62
  and state 119-22
  colonial impact on 80-3
  cultivating castes 52
  hierarchies 11
  high-caste peasant 75-7
  oppression 13
  system 45-7, 49
caste groups, efforts for upward mobility 34
caste society, women's role in formation of 33
Chak-ha-e-Musammati 116-17

Chak-ha-e-Muzakerati 116
Chakravarty, U. 120
Chandhoke, N. 148
Chandra, S. 72, 74
chathi ceremony 93
Childe, Gordon 43
Chowdhry, Prem 22-4, 62
Class,
  and state 115-19
  differentiation 38-9
collective farming 18-19
Collier, J.F. 39
colonial policy, and taluqdari rights 90-2
colonial State Land Acquisition Act 1894 122-3, 125, 130-1, 137-8
conduct code for women 120
Constitution of India, Ninth Schedule 147
Cooper, J.P. 100
Crooke, W. 68
custom, sanctity of 89
customary rights 21

Dalit women 18
Dariao Kunwer, Thakurain 100, 102
daughter
  right of inheritance 23
  socialization of 23
differentiation, process of 45-6
Dreze, J. 26-7
Dumont, L. 98
dwija ceremony 54, 57, 59

egalitarian societies, women's status in 38-9
Engels, L. 37, 43
Etienne, M. 34
Evans-Pritchard, E.E. 34

Faizabad
  taluqdars 93-4
  tenantry 81-2, 85
Fakir and Sannyasi rebellion 51
femininity 50, 61
Fernandes, Walter 125
feudal oppression 13
feudal structures 16
Field of One's Own, A 19
Fisher, Elizabeth 45
food security, in India 15
foraging and hunting gathering tribes, gender equality in 40-2
forest department, tribal women's oppression by 11-12
forest produce, processing of 19
Fox, R.G. 87, 96

gaon samaj lands 151, 154-5, 161, 169
Gazdar, H. 26-7
gender equality 16
gender inequalities, institutionalization of 30
gender justice 16, 31
gender relations,
  agricultural growth and 45-6
  communal to private ownership of land 40-5
  historical evidence 43-5
  implications of growth of hierarchies for 34
  manual labour undervaluation 46-8
  process of differentiation and 45-6
  transformation in 40-8
Gilmartin, D. 92
Goody, J. 87, 100
gram sabha land 132, 151, 154-5, 161, 169
grass-roots organizations 19
grass-roots women's organization 13
grihastha 138-40

Habib, Irfan 67
Hanafi law 98
Hasan, Amir 152, 164
Hasan Raza Saiiyid vs. *Nawab Basti Begam* 103
Hastings, Warren 51

Herring 145
Hindu Mahasabha 50
Hindu Succession Act of 1956 22, 24
households gender dimensions 19
households resources, gender division of 17
hunting gathering Mbuti, Communal Mode among 36
Husain, Syed Baqar 101
Husain, Syed Ghazzafer 101
Husain Baksh 98

Ibbetson, D.C.J. 93
Indian Regulation IV 89
inheritance, patrilineal form of 13
Iroquoi's society, women status in 38

Jafri, S.N.A. 69-70, 72, 81
Jaiswal, S. 42, 45-9, 58-9, 61
jajmani relationships 73
janeo movement 53, 59
Jassal, Smita Tewari 77-8, 82, 87
Jatapu of Andhra Pradesh, gender relations among 41
Jayaswal, Ganga Prasad 59-60
jhum cultivation 42
jurabant principle 98
jural-familial dichotomy 38

Kalwar Kshatriya Mahasabha 58
Kalwars, women's labour in 58-61
Kanyamanoranjan 61
karewa custom 22
Karve, I. 44
Khan, Rashid 118
Khasis of Meghalaya, gender relations among 41
khudkasht peasants 68, 71-4, 77-80, 85
Kiernan, V.G. 87
Klass, Morton 39-40
Kosambi, D.D. 43-4, 152
Kozlowski, G.C. 105
Krishnamurti Foundation Trust 123-5, 131-7
Kshatriyaization process 49
Kulke, H. 49
Kumar, A. 18, 55, 83
Kurmi caste, women's labour in 56-7
Kurmi Sangh 56
Kurmi women, agricultural abilities 70-1
Kusasi of north-eastern Ghana 36

Lal, C.B. 94
Lamphere, L. 37
land, women's rights to 11-27
Land Acquisition Act of 1891 122
Land Alienation Act of 1894 30, 110
land availability for redistribution 16-18
land distribution programme 145
land grants, to women in Mughal state 115-19
land holding,
  area owned by classes 26
  average size of household ownership 27
  by classes 26
  fragmentation of 16
  land reform and redistribution drive 31
  landless and semi-landless households 27
  pattern of 25-7
Land Management Committee 154-5
land ownership, communal to private ownership 40-5
land redistribution drive 31
land reforms 16-17, 31
land to the tiller slogan 16
land tenure, historicity of 13
Landes, Joan 112
landless Dalit women 18
landlessness, problem of 16-17, 30
layered rights 91
Leacock, E. 34, 38-9, 48
Lerche, Jens 132-3
Lerner, Gerda 25, 43

Levi-Strauss, C. 34
Lievelsky, G. 112
Lovedu, Kin Corporate Mode among 36
Ludden, David 65
Lyall, A. 96-7

madad-e-maash grants 121
madad-e-maash tenure 116
Mahajan Hitkarni Sabha 58
Mangal Dev Visharad Committee 155
manual labour, undervaluation of 46-8
marginalization, process of 30
marginalized landless women, study on 144-66
  banjar zamin and 159-62
  bondedness 162-6
  focus of 148-50
  indebtedness 162-6
  patta holders 157-9, 169-70
  pattas without *kabza* 153-7
  setting of 150-3
marriage alliances 22, 99-100, 106-8
  among ruling clans 99-100
  spatial distance due to 22
matriarchy, concept of 43-4
matrilineal system, in Kerala 24
Mazumdar, V. 13, 16
Mehta, Deepak 138-9
Meillassoux, C. 34
Menon, A.G. 150
Metcalfe, Thomas R. 78, 90-1, 94
Mies, M. 44, 46, 141
migrant labour 12
Millett, A.F. 91, 93
Mitra, R.H. 24, 144, 159
Morgan, L.H. 87
Mughal state, land grants to women 115-19
mundan ceremony 93
Muslim Julahas 138-40
Muslim peasant women 16

Naarisudasha Pravartak 61
Narada Samhita 59
Nathan, Dev 40, 43, 148
natural resource management 15
Nazir Ahmed vs. *Swami Dayal* 98
Nevill, H.R. 70, 81, 83, 91
New Economic Policy 13
New Farmers Movements 66
north Indian patrilineal communities 22

OBC women 18
Ojibwa society, women status in 38
Operation Barga 145
Oudh Policy 90-2

Padma Purana 59
pahikasht peasants 68, 73-4, 78
Pankaj, H.S. 154, 156, 158
pat marriage 120
Patnaik, Utsa 66, 73, 152
patriarchy 41-2, 44-5
patrilineal communities 22
patrilineal societies, inheritance rights in 22-4
pattas
  conditions for issue of 159-62
  without *kabza* 153-7
  women as holders of 157-9, 169
Pawar, Krishnashankar 54
peasant communities 47-8
peasant differentiation 29, 65-88
  begari and 83-5
  by caste 71-2
  caste factor in 74-5
  colonial impact on caste 80-3
  colonial rule consequence 77-80
  from peasant to tenants at will 77-80
  high caste peasants 75-7
  in Awadh 65-88
  khudkasht peasants advantages 72-4

residence factor in 67-72
peasant women 13, 15-16, 19, 29, 34, 66-8, 85
labour undervaluation of 34
peasantry, differentiation within 66
peasants uprisings of 1920s 88
Peshwa state 119-22
Pinch, W. 51-4
Plunkett, Frances T. 95, 98, 100
Poitevin, G. 49, 65
Poulantzas, N. 113
poverty alleviation scheme 12
power, gender nature of distribution of 12
power and resource system, women marginalization in 34
primogeniture, tradition and history 95-7, 99-100, 102, 110
private property, concept of 17
Privy Council 104
productive resources
communal ownership of 37
women's access to 40
women's subordination anthropological insights into 36-40
Punjab Laws Act 1872 92
purity and pollution theory 48

Raghunath Koonwer, Thakurain 104
Rai, S. 112, 114
Rairkar, H. 49, 65, 144
Rajput peasants 76-7
Ramanand Koonwer, Thakurain 104
Ramchandra, Baba 56-7, 83-4, 104
Ramcharitmanas 59
Ramnandi *sampradaya* 52
Ramnathan 130-1
Rana, K. 36
Rao, M.S.A. 53
Rao, N. 36
Reddy, N. 145
Risley, H.H. 52
Rosaldo, M.Z. 37
Roy, S. 80-1, 89, 99
ruling clans, affinity and nature of alliances among 97-102

Sacks, Karen 36-7
sacred thread ceremonies 52
Sah, Rustam 100, 106
sanads 91-2, 102
sangathan movement 51
sangathans 13
Sanskritization process, and women 28, 35, 49-61
Santhals,
gender relations in 41-2
witch hunting among 41
Sarai Mohana village
gendered analysis 141-3
impact of loss of village land on women of 137-41
impact of state policy on 110, 113-43
Land Acquisition Act in 125, 130-1
land conflict in 123-4, 131-7
land holdings in 126-9
population by caste and occupation 124-5
sources of land conflict in 131-7
Sardamoni, K. 24-5
Sarma, M. 165
Scheduled Areas and Scheduled Tribes Commission 164
Seabrook, J. 150
secure tenancy 12, 55
Sen, Smita 61
Shankar, K. 155
Sharma, M. 44, 50, 60, 62, 139
shikmi (sub-tenants) 77-9
Shri Nav Yuvak Haihay-Kshatriya Hitkarini Sabha 60
shuddhi movement 50-1
Singh, Bisheshwar Baksh 104
Singh, D. 14, 42
Singh, Madho Pratap 100, 139

Singh, Mohinder 134, 139
Singh, Ram Swarup 104
Singh, Rameshar Baksh 102
Sinha, Pradhan V.K. 123
Skanda Purana 59
slash and burn agriculture 41
social reform, and upward mobility 48-56
sons and daughters, right in patrilineal property 23
South Asia, women's rights in landed property in 22
Srinivas, M.N. 49, 51
Srivastava, M. 134
state and,
  caste 119-22
  class 115-19
Sur, Sher Shah 93
Swaminathan, M.S. 15, 42
swidden agriculture 41

taluqdar 88-98, 101-2, 108
  of Faizabad 93-4
  peasant relations 79-80, 88
  response to Succession Act of 1869 101-2
taluqdari rights, colonial policy and 90-2
Taluqdari Succession Act of 1869 30
taluqdari women
  implication of Succession Act of 1869 102-5
  social and political impact on 105-8
  status of 30
taluqdari women, social and political impact on 105-9
tenancy rights, in agricultural land 23
Thirsk, J. 87
Thompson, E.P. 87, 90
Thukral, E.G. 148
tilak 93
Tinker, I. 36
Tod, James 96, 100
Trautmann, T.R. 107
tribal women, status of 11, 13

upper-caste women 18
usar land 157
Uttar Pradesh, land holding patterns of 25-7

Vaishnavism 51, 59
varna theory 47
varnasamkara theory 48

wage labour 12
wajib-ul-arz 98, 158
Waylen, G. 113, 115
Wazir Mohammed vs. *Har Pershad* 103
wedding celebrations 106-8
Whitehead, A. 36
widows,
  implications of Succession Act of 1869 103-5
  remarriage 120
  right to patrilineal property 24
  voices of 162
witch hunting 41
women,
  access to credit 20
  access to land 15
  access to productive resources 18, 40
  biological theories of 34
  bondedness 162-6
  conduct code for 120
  constitutional guarantees in favour of 22
  contributions in agriculture 17
  control over land and productive resources 12
  denial of access to land 63
  dependence 11
  dependence within families 16
  destitution 20-1
  efficiency 20
  empowerment 16-17, 19-21, 144

enabling challenges to male oppression 20-1
equality 20
gender inequalities 20-1
gender oppression 62
impact of state liberalization policies on 114
impoverishment 11
indebtedness 162-6
individual ownerships of land 15
initiators of agricultural revolution 15
insecurity 11
involvement in agriculture 34
joint and collective ownership and farming 17
land-based productive activities 19
land grants to 115-19
landlessness 16-17, 113-43
management of natural resources 19
marginalization of 15, 30, 34, 144-66
movement 145, 147
Mughal state's land grants to 115-19
oppression 11-12
ownership of land and productive resources 12
participation in productive activity 28
patta holders 157-9
property rights 114
responsibility for housework and child care 20
right to land 11-27
risks arising from marital break-down 20-1
role in agrarian production 29
role in production 34
Sanskritization and 28
security against poverty 20
social empowerment 17
socio-historical probings into right to land 11-27
state and landless women 113-43
state-centric approach to 18
status of 11, 13, 20, 37-9
subordination 21, 36-40
Succession Act of 1869, impact on 102-5
suppression of 33
as tillers 16
title to lands 16
undervaluation of economic contributions of 16
village lands loss, impact on 137-41
vulnerability to violence 20
welfare issue 20

women's labour
agricultural operation in Awadh 69-86
Kalwars 58-61
Kurmi caste case 56-7
Sanskritization context 48-61
social reform 48-56
upward mobility 48-56
utilization of 29

women's mobilization 19
women's movement 16
women's subordination theories of 28

Yadava movement 53
yagnopavita ritual 59
Yanagisako, S.J. 39

Zainab, Mussammat 117
Zamindari Abolition Act 27, 134, 155